THE MAZE OF
BELIEFS

HECTOR CANTU KALIFA

ACKNOWLEDGMENTS

All my thanks and all the glory go to Jesus, who went out to search for me and found me, just like in the parable of the lost sheep.

Thank you, God the Father, for sending us your Son Jesus to save us and show us the way to you.

Thank you, Jesus, for giving yourself for us on the cross and for giving us the Holy Spirit as our guide and comfort.

Thank you, Holy Spirit, for revealing the Truth to me, illuminating my path, and giving me the strength to continue each day with faith and hope.

Thank you, Divine Trinity, for your infinite love and your limitless mercy.

Love them all!

All glory to you, Lord Jesus.

CONTENTS

PART 1

THE TRUTH
OF OUR ORIGIN

INTRO

There comes a time in life when we ask ourselves profound questions: Who is God? Where do we come from? What is our purpose in this life?

As believers, we accept that God is the Creator of the universe and everything that exists. But even with that certainty, new questions arise: Who created God? What does it mean for God to be a Divine Being? What existed before time, space, or matter?

These and other similar questions had always troubled me. I sought answers in logic, New Age ideas, topics like the law of attraction, chakra meditation ... I thought I understood the "universe" and its energies, until one day, while praying and praising Jesus, the Holy Spirit arrived like a powerful wind, covering me with an energy of indescribable love.

My body trembled, my skin prickled, tears flowed uncontrollably, and a single phrase filled my mind: "Forgive me, Jesus." His presence was alive, real, enveloping me with an intensity that healed my soul and renewed my entire being.

I never before experienced anything so profound, so pure, so vibrant, not even during my chakra-focused meditations or breathing techniques.

Then I knew for sure: *it was the Holy Spirit.* That experience completely transformed me.

I asked the Holy Spirit to reveal to me the lies I had believed, and I began to have inner visions. I understood that many of my beliefs weren't true, but rather human assumptions unrooted in God. It's as if I were trying to tell you what your favorite hobby is without knowing you, without knowing how you think or what you're like. What I would say would be either a lie or a mere assumption. I had tried to understand my Creator without asking Him directly. The Holy Spirit showed me the truth.

Since then, some people have asked me: "How is it possible that you once spoke with such certainty about the New Age, and now you say with the same conviction that the truth is in Jesus?" I answer that there is one small, but significant difference that changed everything: before, I spoke from human knowledge; now I speak from the freedom that only Jesus gave me. This is because it is by believing in Him that I am truly free. As He Himself said: "You will know the truth, and the truth will set you free" (John 8:32). That was the difference. It wasn't a theory; it was a real experience of inner freedom that transformed my life.

This experience had a profound impact on me. I spent days reflecting on the visions and divine energy I had felt.

From then on, I decided I wouldn't teach anything I hadn't first experienced. I committed myself to knowing God deeply, reading about Jesus, and opening myself completely to the Holy Spirit. That journey changed my life and helped me better understand the Trinity, existence, and my identity as a child of God.

Of course, I don't have all the answers, and I never will. But I no longer focus on what I don't know; I hold fast to what I do know. I know that God is real, that Jesus is risen, and that the Holy Spirit guides and transforms. And that's enough to walk in faith.

The real challenge, however, is not in understanding Divinity, but in connecting with it. There are many energies in this world, but only one is truly Divine. Learning to identify it and allowing oneself to be guided by it is the key to living fully and in communion with God.

To begin this book, we will reflect on the existence of God. We must not allow the unknown to lead us to doubt what we do know. There are four truths that are my starting point:

1. Everything that begins has a cause. The universe had a beginning, so someone started it.

2. The universe is perfectly tuned, with exact laws and conditions that allow life, which implies the existence of an intelligent being.

3. All human beings distinguish between good and evil, which suggests a moral Legislator.

4. Every creation is always external to its creator. A building doesn't build itself; someone must design and erect it. A table doesn't arise spontaneously; someone must shape the wood and assemble it. Similarly, time, matter, and space—that is, the universe itself—could not have created themselves.

If questions arise beyond these certainties, they don't invalidate what we already know; they simply remind us that there is still much to explore and understand. Mystery is not the absence of truth, but an invitation to delve deeper into it.

Stephen Hawking noted that if the expansion rate of the universe had been even slightly different, the universe would not exist as we know it. This seems much more than a coincidence; it suggests deliberate design.

This cause of the universe must be outside of time, matter, and space. Therefore, it must be timeless, immaterial, powerful, intelligent, and personal. Who else can fulfill these characteristics but God?

When asked how to identify the true God, the evidence points to Jesus. Not only did he predict and fulfill his own resurrection—an undeniable supernatural fact—but his life, death, and resurrection aligned remarkably with more than three-hundred Old Testament prophecies, confirming his divine identity.

Seven hundred years before his arrival, the prophet Isaiah described in detail the suffering of the Messiah, mirroring the life of Jesus: despised, rejected, bearing the sins of humanity. Isaiah 53:1-7 is a poignant testimony to this connection: "Who has believed our message… He was despised and rejected by mankind, a man of suffering, and familiar with pain. Like one from whom people hide their faces he was despised, and we held him in low esteem… But he was pierced for our transgressions, he was crushed for our iniquities; the punishment that brought us peace was on him, and by his wounds we are healed."

The convergence of prophecy and fulfillment in Jesus reinforces his identity as the promised Messiah and, by extension, as the Creator God who became incarnate among us.

The evidence for Jesus's resurrection is overwhelming. The empty tomb, guarded by Roman soldiers and sealed with a large rock, attests that Jesus's body was not stolen. Why did the Pharisees, fearing a false resurrection, not present the body to refute the disciples? Furthermore, it is unlikely that the disciples, filled with fear after the crucifixion, would have dared to steal the body and confront the authorities.

The resurrection transformed the apostles. They went from fear and doubt to becoming courageous preachers, willing to face persecution and death for proclaiming the truth of the resurrection. Who would die for a lie? This radical transformation can only be explained by a real encounter with the risen Christ.

But the most powerful evidence is Jesus's ongoing impact on the world. Centuries later, his miracles, his message of love, forgiveness, and hope continue to transform lives, inspire acts of kindness, and heal broken hearts. This enduring influence is a living testimony that the resurrection is not just an event of the past, but a present reality that continues to change the world.

With this, I begin a series of reflections that have guided me toward a deeper understanding of our existence, of God's identity, and how to establish a genuine connection with Him. The chapters are short and to the point, making them easy to read and avoiding the fatigue that long books sometimes produce. My intention is to teach each topic concisely, leaving room for personal reflection.

Of course, I haven't discovered anything revolutionary; these ideas have been around for years. My goal is simply to present them in a different way, hopefully making them more accessible. I recognize that I don't have all the answers. The endless search for "why?" and "how?" inevitably leads us to a point where all we can say is "I don't know." But what I don't know doesn't negate what I do know.

"Jesus answered, 'I am the way and the truth and the life. No one comes to the Father except through me.'"
JOHN 14:6

CHAPTER 1

THE GREAT DIVINE RESTORATION

I magine you're a highly technological creator. You've designed ten intelligent robots that work in your office, assisting you in creating and programming new ideas. You've not only given them intelligence, but also the freedom to make decisions on their own.

Among your various projects, you decided to create a completely new and special version: beautiful and incomparable robots, designed in your image and likeness. This new creation fascinated you so much that you decided to send two of them to a unique and extraordinary place outside your office. This space was beautiful and perfect for them to live, enjoy, and multiply in peace. You had given them intelligence, free will, and, above all, made them similar to you.

At first, these special robots enjoyed a full and happy life in this paradise. They lacked nothing; they experienced peace, love, and gratitude, and spoke to you frequently, recognizing you as their creator.

However, one of the original ten robots, from your office, began to feel jealousy and envy. He couldn't bear the thought that you had created something so beautiful and special and that you had given them such a magnificent place to live. Overcome by envy, he decided to sabotage this new creation. He thought, "If I can't have what they have, I won't let them enjoy it either."

After a long time of planning, the jealous robot found a way to infiltrate and sabotage your creation. He developed and introduced a virus into the systems of the two new robots. This virus was destructive and began to profoundly alter their programming, corrupting their thoughts and erasing the memory of their true identity—that identity that reflected the image and likeness of their creator. The virus was so powerful that it destroyed their original consciousness and forced them to develop a completely distorted identity.

You, as the creator, watched from above. With deep sorrow, you watched as your most beautiful creation, the robots made in your image, deteriorated day after day due to the virus. You had the option to eliminate the envious robot and destroy all the infected robots. However, you valued your original work too highly and decided against it. Destroying your creation would mean conceding a victory to the envious robot, and you wouldn't allow that.

You decided to give it another chance, selecting a family of robots that could start over. You cleaned up the environment and allowed these robots to inhabit it, hoping to restore the initial harmony. However, as time passed, the evil persisted. The virus was still present in the system, and the robots continued to fight and destroy each other.

Meanwhile, the envious robot watched from afar, enjoying what seemed like its ultimate triumph. Although you had expelled it from your immediate surroundings, it continued to influence the contaminated creation. But you, in your infinite wisdom, still had a much grander and more revolutionary plan.

You decided to infuse your own consciousness and supreme power into a special robot that you would send to live among them. This unique robot would be filled with your divine essence and would have the ability to reset the others' programming, remove the virus, and restore the memory of their true original identity. It would remind them that they had been created in the image and likeness of their creator, and thus they would regain their lost peace and love.

You knew perfectly well that by doing so, the robots still under the influence of the jealous robot would attempt to destroy you. However, your plan included that, at the moment of your physical destruction, your consciousness and power would be transmitted to all the robots who chose to believe and trust in you, thus granting them the ability to heal themselves and free themselves from the virus forever.

• • •

This analogy helps us understand, in a simple way, the profound mystery of the Divine Trinity.

- The original creator of all robots represents God the Father.

- The consciousness and supreme power that was introduced into the special robot symbolize the Holy Spirit.

- The special robot who lived among the other robots is Jesus, the Son of God.

The envious robot symbolizes Satan, who, filled with jealousy and hatred, seeks to destroy divine creation.

The virus that infected the robots is a metaphor for original sin, which corrupted our true identity and separated us from our original purpose: to live in harmony and communion with our Creator.

Just as in the analogy the Creator chose to incarnate himself as a robot to save his creation, God the Father sent his Son, Jesus, into the world to redeem us from sin, heal us, and restore our original identity. In the same way, the divine consciousness of the Creator (the Holy Spirit) remains among us, guiding and strengthening us each day on our spiritual journey.

The Holy Trinity is, of course, a profound and complex mystery, but this analogy allows us to more simply understand how God, in his infinite love and mercy, reaches out to us to offer us salvation and eternal life.

Finally, let us remember this powerful verse from Matthew 20:28:

> "Just as the Son of Man did not come to be served, but to serve, and to give his life as a ransom for many."

THE VEIL OF IGNORANCE

I'm lying on the floor with an unbearable ringing in my ears that's giving me a headache. I feel dizzy, as if I've just woken up from an endless dream. I rub my forehead and, little by little, the ringing fades. I try to remember something, but my memory is blank. I don't know who I am, or where I am.

I sit up slowly. I open my eyes... but everything is still dark. I touch my eyelids to make sure they're open. Yes, they are. Yet I can't see anything. Am I blind?

In the distance, I hear whispers. I walk carefully toward them and ask where we are. Two voices answer me kindly: "We're in a large room. We're also blind. No one knows what lies beyond." Apparently, they've been living there for some time.

We spend our days inventing ways to entertain ourselves. The room, though dark, has what it takes to survive. No one hurts us, but we also don't know what's out there.

Until one day, a loud bang shakes the place. I fall to the ground, trembling with fear. It's the first time anything has broken the stillness. We hear one of the walls collapse. We approach and, to our surprise, the wall is gone. We hesitate for a moment, but decide to leave.

Outside, I feel a soft, damp breeze caress my face. I reflexively close my eyes... and then I feel it. A warm light passes through my eyelids. I don't know what it is, but my body shudders with excitement. I stay still, a smile forming on my face. The warmth envelops me. I feel a different, alive energy. It's as if something is awakening inside me.

I can't explain it, but that light brings me peace. My companions beside me are also silent, enjoying the same experience. After a while, we return to the room, our hearts still pounding.

That night, we talked about what we felt. One says it was a person shining a light on us. Another thinks it was an object. I think it was something else... like a living energy. We didn't reach an agreement, but we all shared the same feelings: warmth, peace, joy.

As the days pass, more blind people arrive. We tell them about the light and take them outside to experience it. Each one, upon sensing it, gives their own interpretation. Some say it's a powerful being. Others, that it's the luminous wind. Although everyone describes it differently, the emotion is universal.

But one day, while we were enjoying the light, it suddenly disappeared. We returned to the room, disappointed. Then, a firm voice broke the silence:

"Where do you go? The light is still here."

We stop. Confused, we reply that the light has gone out. The figure approaches. I feel its presence in front of me. Then, a hand touches my eyes.

In that moment... I see.

Colors. Shapes. Life.

An immense forest stretches out before me, illuminated by a golden light that filters through the leaves. Tears spring to my eyes. Finally, I understand: the darkness we lived in wasn't real. It was only a shadow hiding what had always been there.

The man smiles and says, "The light didn't disappear. You just had to open your eyes."

Some of my companions also accept his touch and come. Others, fearful, refuse. They prefer to remain in the known darkness rather than venture into the unknown.

Those of us who see the light follow man along the shining path. Those who don't, stay behind, clinging to the shadows.

* * *

The warmth that caressed them was not just a physical sensation, but the awakening of a higher reality that had always been there waiting for them. God.

When a soul has lived its entire life in darkness, even the smallest glimmer becomes a miracle. That light was a revelation to them, like when a hardened heart feels true love for the first time. Each tried to explain what they had felt, but their descriptions were based on imagination, not vision. That didn't make them false, just incomplete.

The same is true of our different ways of understanding God. Some imagine Him as a person, others as an energy or a universal presence. But the truth is that, like the sun, God cannot be fully described by those who have not yet opened the eyes of their soul. Only those who receive the touch of the Holy Spirit can see beyond the shadows and experience God as He truly is.

The darkness surrounding the blind was only a shadow, an illusion. In our spiritual life, that shadow is evil, ignorance, sin... everything that prevents us from seeing the eternal light. The unknown man, who represents Jesus, came to dispel that shadow and open our eyes. He didn't force anyone; he simply offered his touch, his truth, his light.

Those who accepted that touch began to see. Their world, once limited to eternal blackness, was filled with color, beauty, and meaning. Those who rejected the touch remained trapped in their own willful darkness. Not because the light wasn't there, but because they chose not to see it.

That spiritual warmth touches our lives when we pray, when we are forgiven, when we forgive, when we serve with humility, or simply when we love. That warmth is God.

As the Scripture says in 1 John 4:8:

"Whoever does not love does not know God, because God is love."

And later:

"No one has ever seen God; but if we love one another, God lives in us and his love is made complete in us. This is how we know that we live in him and he in us: He has given us of his Spirit." (1 John 4:12-13).

The light is there. It has always been. The question is: Will you allow Jesus to touch your eyes and reveal it to you? Because once He does, you will no longer walk in the dark, but will be guided by the light of divine love, which dispels the shadows and leads you toward the fullness of life.

CHAPTER 3

SPARKS FROM GOD'S EXPANSION

Many of us have learned that we are children of God if we are baptized. However, this teaching can raise profound questions: Why do we need baptism to be recognized as children of our Creator? What does it really mean to be children of God, and how can we be brothers and sisters to all human beings?

My intention is to reflect on these questions and help you understand that, although we all come from God, He grants us the freedom to decide whether we want to accept His love and be adopted as His children. This act of spiritual adoption makes us heirs of a divine legacy, with authority and power in Christ.

This divine power we inherit is not just a concept, but a reality that Jesus made clear in Luke 10:19: "I have given you authority to trample on snakes and scorpions and to overcome all the power of the enemy; nothing will harm you." This authority allows us to live in victory, overcome the obstacles of the world, and align ourselves with God's eternal purpose: to live in fulfillment and happiness with Him.

Imagine a full jug of water in front of you. When you tilt it, the water flows to the ground. When it's completely emptied, we see something revealing: in the center, where the water directly fell, a large pool forms; around it, puddles of varying sizes appear; and further away, we see small, scattered drops. Although they appear separate, all these drops come from the same jug.

In the same way, God—the divine and conscious Being—decided to create the entire universe. In creating humanity, He made us in His image and likeness. We are like those scattered drops: distinct, yet all from one origin.

As Genesis 1:26–27 declares:

"Then God said, *'Let Us make man in Our image, according to Our likeness;* and let them rule over the fish of the sea and the birds of the sky, and over the cattle and over all the earth, and over every creeping thing that creeps on the earth.' So God created man in His own image; in the image of God He created him; male and female He created them."

THE SEPARATION FROM THE SOURCE

In the beginning, we lived in perfect connection with God, in peace and harmony, because He is Love and there is no evil in Him. Yet in creating us, He gave us free will.

That freedom carried the possibility of disobedience, and so it happened: original sin broke our communion with God. At that moment, we handed over our authority to the devil.

What does it mean to "give authority" to the devil? Think of a father who has authority over his children. That authority is broken when the children disobey. Spiritually, it is the same: by sinning, we obey evil and move away from Love, because light and darkness cannot coexist. By rejecting God, we surrender ground to the enemy.

That is why Satan could say to Jesus: *"All this authority has been given to me"* (Luke 4:6). That authority was given to him by us when we sinned and obeyed Satan. Sin is the gravest offense against God, and divine justice demands a consequence—condemnation.

LOVE, JUSTICE, AND MERCY

You might ask: If God is Love, why does condemnation exist?

Because true love includes justice.

Imagine you have two children, and one of them hits his sister. You love them both deeply, yet you know you must protect and defend your daughter. You give your son a consequence, not out of lack of love, but because justice is part of true love.

Now, if your son repents and sincerely asks for forgiveness, you, as a merciful father, will forgive him. Here, love joins with mercy and justice.

In the same way, when Adam and Eve sinned, the consequence was condemnation… but God, in His mercy, did not want that to be our destiny. That is why He sent His Son, Jesus, to pay our debt and open the way back home.

PAYING THE DEBT

Imagine you suffer a terrible accident caused by someone else. Stepping out of the car, you see it is completely wrecked, almost beyond repair. Then you realize the other person has no insurance, no money, and no way to compensate you.

Moved by compassion, you decide to cover all the costs yourself, demanding nothing from the guilty party. You say: "Don't worry, I will pay it all." The damage is already done—someone has to assume responsibility.

That is exactly what God did with us: He took on our debt by sending Jesus to die in our place. It was the greatest act of love imaginable.

Through baptism, we receive this gift: the Holy Spirit descends upon us, unites us with the body of Christ, and reconciles us with the Father. It is not just a ritual, but a transforming encounter, as Jesus said:

"Unless one is born of water and the Spirit, he cannot enter the kingdom of God" (John 3:5).

Peter explained it this way:

> *"Repent, and be baptized every one of you… and you will receive the gift of the Holy Spirit"* (Acts 2:38).

When God calls us to account, I will be able to point to Jesus and say: "I owe You nothing; He paid for me," fulfilling what Scripture says:

> *"Having canceled the record of debt that stood against us… He set it aside, nailing it to the cross"* (Colossians 2:14).

A SPIRITUAL INHERITANCE

In baptism we receive gifts and spiritual authority. Paul explains it like this:

> "And if we are children, then we are heirs—heirs of God and co-heirs with Christ…" (Romans 8:17).

Jesus Himself declared:

> "I have given you authority to trample on snakes and scorpions and to overcome all the power of the enemy; nothing will harm you" (Luke 10:19).

What does this mean? These are strong words, whose depth we often fail to grasp. Being heirs of God is not a decorative phrase; it is a spiritual reality.

To be heirs of God means to receive forgiveness, authority over the enemy, and access to the Kingdom. If we are co-heirs with Christ and He gives us His authority, then we have the right to exercise His power in the world to overcome evil and the enemy, with all its temptations and consequences.

This authority—when lived in faith in Christ—allows us to live in victory, free from evil, from worry, from anger, and from life's storms. It gives us power to overcome the obstacles of the world and to live in peace.

AUTHORITY AND POWER

Power is the capacity; authority is the legal right to exercise it.

Here's an example: a black belt in martial arts has the physical power to stop someone, but not the authority to arrest them—that authority belongs to the police. Spiritually, many have "power" (knowledge, gifts), but only in the name of Jesus can one exercise legitimate authority to defeat the enemy.

If a Christian faces a case of spiritual oppression—for instance, his daughter has constant nightmares and feels a dark presence—and he only prays silently, his words may not have the same impact. But when he stands firm and declares with authority: *"In the name of Jesus, I command every unclean spirit to leave and never return,"* he is exercising the power and authority that Christ has given him, and the enemy cannot resist.

That power and authority are received in baptism, when we become children of God.

A CALL FOR ALL

Every human being has a soul created by God. That soul needs to return to Him through Jesus, by accepting our identity as children through baptism.

If we understand that we all come from God and were created in His image, why criticize, envy, or mistreat others? By harming our neighbor, we also wound God, who dwells in each person.

Jesus calls us to love our neighbor as ourselves, because we were made in God's image and likeness, and those who are baptized are part of the same body.

> "Just as a body, though one, has many parts, but all its many parts form one body, so it is with Christ. For we were all baptized by one Spirit so as to form one body— whether Jews or Gentiles, slave or free—and we were all given the one Spirit to drink." (1 Corinthians 12:12-13)

This is our true identity and our greatest inheritance: to live united in Christ, as one body, reflecting the love of the One who created us.

CHAPTER 4

CHILDREN BY BLOOD

A shepherd was walking through the countryside when he found a distraught sheep bleating desperately. Her little lamb had died, the victim of a wild animal attack. A few meters away, he found a lone lamb crying inconsolably: its mother had suffered the same fate.

Both had lost something invaluable. The ewe had milk, but lacked a child to feed. The lamb, on the other hand, was hungry, but no longer had a mother to sustain it.

However, sheep never suckle a lamb that is not their own. Their maternal instinct responds only to the scent of their own offspring. A foreign lamb feels strange, unfamiliar, and even hostile to them.

But the shepherd knew exactly what to do.

He took the blood of the lamb that had died and smeared it on the body of the little orphan. As he brought the blood-covered lamb closer to the sheep, something extraordinary happened: the sheep sniffed deeply, and its heart recognized that scent. The little one was no longer a stranger, but carried the scent of her son. Without hesitation, the sheep opened her heart, accepted him, fed him, and protected him as if he had always been her own.

This story is not just a metaphor; it is fact.

Since ancient times, shepherds have used this method to convince a sheep to adopt an orphan lamb. By covering the orphan lamb with the blood of its deceased child, the sheep accepts and adopts the baby as its own. It's an ancient practice that has been passed down from generation to generation.

It is no coincidence that God, knowing the profound symbolism of this image, called Jesus "the Lamb of God." John 1:29 we read: "The next day John saw Jesus coming toward him and said, 'Look, the Lamb of God, who takes away the sin of the world!'"

Just as that shepherd covered the orphan lamb with the blood of the one who had died, God used the precious blood of Jesus, His Son, to adopt us spiritually and save us from condemnation. We were like orphan lambs, wandering and stained by sin. Our communion with God had been broken since Adam and Eve sinned, and we no longer had a right to His presence or His inheritance.

However, God the Father, in His infinite mercy, sent Jesus, His perfect Lamb, to sacrifice Himself for us. When He poured His divine blood upon us, something changed forever:

Now when God looks at us, He no longer sees our past, our sins, or our wounds. He sees only the blood of His beloved Son covering us.

This radically changes our identity and our relationship with Him. Ephesians 2:13 reminds us: "But now in Christ Jesus you who once were far away have been brought near by the blood of Christ."

And Hebrews 10:19 states: "Therefore, brothers and sisters, since we have confidence to enter the Most Holy Place by the blood of Jesus."

Thanks to Jesus's sacrifice, we are no longer strangers or spiritual orphans. We are adopted children, covered and transformed by His blood, which grants us a new divine identity.

As 1 Peter 1:18-19 says: "For you know that it was not with perishable things such as silver or gold that you were redeemed from the empty way of life handed down to you from your ancestors, *but with the precious blood of Christ, a lamb without blemish or defect.*"

And the messianic prophecy of Isaiah 53:7 states: "He was oppressed and afflicted, yet he did not open his mouth; he was led like a lamb to the slaughter, and as a sheep before its shearers is silent, so he did not open his mouth."

Jesus faithfully fulfilled this prophecy, offering himself without resistance for our redemption.

Finally, Revelation 12:11 concludes with a powerful statement: "They triumphed over him by the blood of the Lamb and by the word of their testimony; they did not love their lives so much as to shrink from death."

Through the blood of the Lamb, we are now adopted, nourished by His grace, and sustained eternally by His love.

CHAPTER 5

ONE CHOICE, ONE PATH, ONE DOOR

✝

In this chapter, I've compiled some analogies that helped me better understand the spiritual path. I hope they resonate with you as well.

THE WRONG GATE CAN LEAD YOU ASTRAY

Imagine you're rushing to the airport, in a hurry because your flight is about to depart. After passing through security, you look for your gate. However, when you check your pass, you notice something alarming: it's blank. You don't know which gate will take you home, and anxiety begins to invade you.

Desperate, you meet up with a friend. You ask him which is the correct gate, but he replies, "Any gate." Confused, you follow his advice and board a random plane. Upon landing, you discover you're not home. Perhaps you've arrived in a dangerous area, dodging conflict and danger, or maybe you're stuck in a freezing cold place without proper clothing. The reality is that, although well-intentioned, your friend's advice didn't help you. This could have been avoided if someone had pointed you toward the correct gate from the start.

This analogy represents what happens today to those who believe that any religion or path leads to heaven or God. Our true home is heaven, the place where we belong because we were created in the image and likeness of God. But do all paths really lead there?

Jesus is clear when he tells us: "Jesus answered, 'I am the way and the truth and the life. No one comes to the Father except through me.'" (John 14:6)

Jesus isn't just another option; *He's the only door to our true home.* Choosing any other path can distance us from the destination where we truly belong.

A DECISIVE CROSSROADS

Imagine now that you're driving down a road that splits into two directions. It's a crucial decision, but you don't have a map or clear signs indicating the right path. In the distance, you see two figures: one is alive, and the other, obviously, is dead.

Which one would you ask for the right path? The answer is obvious: you would ask someone who is alive. Only someone who is alive can guide you with certainty.

In the spiritual realm, Jesus is the only one who can do it. Unlike important figures like Buddha, Muhammad, or Moses, whose bodies remain buried in the earth, Jesus was resurrected. His tomb is empty. His victory over death proves that He has the power and wisdom to guide us.

THE ONLY DOOR

Jesus clearly said, "I am the gate; whoever enters through me will be saved. They will come in and go out, and find pasture." (John 10:9).

He is the only legitimate access to the Father. Taking alternative paths can lead us to spiritually erroneous destinations, far from God.

Every day we face important decisions. Choosing the right door isn't a matter of luck, but of recognizing the truth revealed in Jesus. He didn't leave us in uncertainty; He Himself is the sure guide to God.

When you have to decide, ask yourself: Am I following the living? Am I entering through the right door?

WHY IS JESUS OUR SALVATION?

Jesus is our salvation because God, in his infinite love, decided to personally take payment for our sins. He sent his Son Jesus to bear our guilt and offer us salvation.

But salvation from what?

Since God is love, He must also be just. True love includes justice.

When Adam and Eve committed original sin, something was broken in creation—a spiritual damage whose consequence was condemnation. But God, in His mercy, did not want that to be our destiny. That's why He sent His Son, Jesus, to pay the debt with His life, to restore what had been lost, and to open the way back home.

Through our sins, we broke our relationship with Him and caused irreparable harm. This harm, according to divine justice, had to be repaid, because God is just. However, He is also merciful, and instead of making us carry that burden, He said, "I'll take care of it."

He decided to pay that debt Himself by sending Jesus to die in our place, to bear the punishment we deserved. This divine act was the greatest display of love imaginable.

By dying for us, He opened the only way back to the Father. *You just have to accept it.* It is available to anyone who believes in Him and receives Him as their Lord and Savior.

WHAT HAPPENS TO THOSE WHO DO NOT BELIEVE IN JESUS CHRIST?

God respects our freedom. Those who reject Jesus in life, even if they were good people, must face divine justice and answer for their own spiritual debt.

Some may have a chance at purification in Purgatory, a temporary state before entering God's presence. But those who accept Jesus and die without sin (that is, reconciled with God) are guaranteed direct entry to heaven.

God made it clear in His Word:

> Jeremiah 31:34: "For I will *forgive their wickedness and will remember their sins no more.*"

> Isaiah 43:25: "I, even I, am he who blots out your transgressions, for my own sake, and *remembers your sins no more.*"

> Micah 7:18-19: "Who is a God like you, who pardons sin and forgives the transgression of the remnant of his inheritance? (…) you will tread our sins underfoot and *hurl all our iniquities into the depths of the sea.*"

Hebrews 10:17: "*Their sins and lawless acts I will remember no more.*"

If God forgives us and forgets our sins, we have no outstanding debt to Him. Jesus already paid for our sins on the cross, and if we accept His sacrifice, we can be certain that our salvation is assured.

On the other hand, those who die without accepting Jesus have an outstanding debt.

The decision is yours.

God doesn't impose his love or his salvation. He offers you the way, but it's up to you to decide whether you accept it or not.

Will you enter through the door that leads to eternal life, or will you follow an uncertain path?

Your salvation is in your hands.

CHAPTER 6

EATING TO LIVE ETERNALLY

✝

In the chapter "Sparks of God's Expansion," I mentioned that by receiving the Eucharist, we connect directly with the Creator. In this reflection, I want to delve deeper into that idea through an analogy that reveals the vital importance of nourishing our souls.

Humans have bodies that need essential elements to survive: air, water, and food. Without them, the body weakens to the point of not functioning. But simply consuming them isn't enough: their quality matters. Breathing polluted air damages the lungs. Drinking unclean water can make us sick. Eating processed foods harms our health. On the other hand, when we choose clean air, clean water, and nutritious food, our bodies become stronger, energized, and able to live more fully.

The same thing happens with the soul. As Teilhard de Chardin said: "We are not human beings having a spiritual experience, but spiritual beings having a human experience."

If we are, in essence, spiritual beings, how do we properly nourish our spirits?

Today, there are many ways to "nourish" spirituality, religions, philosophies, techniques, and meditations among others. But just as not all foods are good for the body, not all practices nourish the soul and spirit in a healthy way.

There is one fundamental thing about the spiritual: there is only one Creator. He is the source of our existence and the only truly essential nourishment for our soul. We come from Him, and it is in *Him that our soul finds its fulfillment, its purity, its strength, and its salvation.*

WHICH OF ALL THE SPIRITUAL FOODS IS THE BEST FOR OUR SOUL?

Jesus clearly answered this need in John 6:51-58: "I am the living bread that came down from heaven. Whoever eats this bread will live forever… Whoever eats my flesh and drinks my blood has eternal life… For my flesh is real food and my blood is real drink… whoever feeds on this bread will live forever."

Jesus didn't speak figuratively. He presents himself as the true food: whoever receives it remains in Him and lives forever. Only He offers not only spiritual strength, but eternal life.

Other spiritual methods or "foods" may provide momentary relief, inspiration, or emotional well-being, but none offer what Jesus offers: union with God and eternal salvation.

WHAT HAPPENS WHEN WE DON'T NOURISH OUR SOULS WITH JESUS?

Many seek energy in alternative spiritual practices: Reiki, Buddhism, crystals, Eastern meditations. These may generate sensations or moments of peace, but they rarely bring lasting satisfaction. Like a body that survives on junk food, the soul remains hungry. Those who do not nourish themselves with the eternal end up endlessly searching.

That's the big difference: Jesus's energy is eternal, healing, and deeply satisfying. When you experience his true love, your soul is filled. You no longer need to keep searching. Restlessness disappears. You've come home.

COMMUNION: THE SUPREME GIFT

In the Eucharist, Jesus offers us his body and blood as true nourishment for the soul. This sacred act is not only a symbolic remembrance of his sacrifice, but a real and living union with his divinity.

Upon receiving it, we enter into communion with the Creator. It is at this moment that the soul is strengthened, purified, and connected directly to the source of life.

The devil can disguise himself as light and manipulate other forms of spirituality. But the divine energy of Jesus is impenetrable, incorruptible, and infinitely more powerful. Only He has the power to protect us from evil that other practices, religions, or artifacts cannot offer.

AN INVITATION TO RETURN TO THE SOURCE

Therefore, do not be afraid to praise God or receive Jesus in Communion. It is the greatest gift we have been given: His body and blood, offered to give us life, salvation, and freedom. Don't let shame, doubt, or the judgment of others keep you from the purest and most sacred food.

Allow the love of Jesus to fill you completely.

Let the Holy Spirit flood you. And you will experience a fullness and peace that no other source can give you.

Your soul will return home.

CHAPTER 7

THE RACE OF LIFE

Imagine that your entire life you've eaten junk food, never exercised, or cared about taking care of your body. Your parents never taught you how to eat well or exercise because they didn't either. The years go by, and you start to gain considerable weight. By the time you reach fifty, your body begins to feel the toll of years of poor habits: your knees and lower back hurt constantly. You walk with difficulty because your hip is bothering you. You can no longer stand for long periods of time because the pain in your knees becomes unbearable.

Tired of your physical condition and the discomfort that prevents you from moving properly, you decide to take matters into your own hands and see a nutritionist. They teach you, little by little, how to eliminate certain unhealthy foods and how to gradually begin exercising. They guide you on what and how much to eat, and what exercises to perform. Each week, they adjust your diet and increase the intensity of your exercise, replacing bad habits with healthier options.

A month later, you start to notice significant changes: you've lost several pounds, the pain in your knees is lessening, your back feels stronger, and you can now stand for longer periods of time without discomfort. This progress motivates you to keep going. You become more committed to your diet, increase the intensity of your workouts, and, before you know it, you're already jogging.

Three months later, you've almost reached your ideal weight. The pain in your knees and back is completely gone. You feel light, agile, and have renewed energy. You can now run effortlessly, and the physical well-being you experience inspires you to set a new goal: running a full marathon.

For the next six months, you continue training with discipline. You eat well, increase your endurance, and strengthen your body. Finally, ten months after starting this process, you run a marathon and finish it with a smile from ear to ear.

A year ago you could barely walk without pain, and now you've managed to complete a 42-kilometer run. You feel happy, satisfied, and proud of yourself.

This is what happens with our spiritual life.

We often live far from Jesus, feeding on the noise of the world, negative thoughts, and unhealed wounds. Everything seems bearable for a while, but eventually our soul begins to take its toll: lack of peace, anger, anxiety, emptiness. We feel lost and directionless.

And so, like the one who sought out the nutritionist, we seek the true guide to heal the soul: Jesus. He is the one who restores us, teaches us to live anew, and transforms us from within.

Other spiritual paths may offer momentary comfort, but only Jesus can give you deep and lasting peace, a peace that doesn't depend on circumstances. Once you begin to walk with Him, you feel your inner being change: more patience, more hope, more love. You discover that you can talk to Him as if you were speaking to a close friend, because Jesus is alive, present, and close.

As your relationship with Jesus deepens, your spirit is strengthened. You discover a peace that endures even in the midst of storms. The same peace Jesus displayed when he slept in the boat while the sea was raging (Mark 4:38-39).

And when your soul experiences this transformation, you feel like a marathon runner who crosses the finish line: full of life, joy, and fulfillment.

Now think about this: Who brings greater joy, the one who has always led a healthy life, or the one who, without guidance or good habits, manages to transform their life and run a marathon? The answer is clear: the one who overcame the greatest obstacles. And the true friend, the one who has always run marathons, far from feeling envious, is happy to see his companion catch up and run alongside him.

This is how God is with us.

Those who never knew the faith or who strayed from Jesus but returned and surrendered to Him caused immense joy in heaven. And those who already walk with Jesus, far from feeling jealous, joyfully celebrate His return. Because in the end, we all share the same goal: eternal life.

Jesus himself taught it in the parable of the prodigal son: "But while he was still a long way off, his father saw him and was filled with compassion for him; he ran to his son, threw his arms around him and kissed him" (Luke 15:20).

CHAPTER 8

THE CLOSER YOU GET, THE GREATER HE BECOMES

W e've heard much about the greatness of Jesus and his infinite goodness. God, in his immense majesty, chose to become incarnate in a human being—Jesus—to save us through his sacrifice on the cross. By rising again, he not only conquered sin and death, but also left us a priceless gift: the Holy Spirit, who guides, strengthens, and empowers us to overcome eternal damnation.

But how can we understand the magnitude of his greatness?

The only way is to get closer to Him.

Imagine flying in an airplane and looking down on a building from above. It looks small, insignificant. The further you get, the more its size diminishes. However, as you get closer, the building grows larger before your eyes. When you stand directly below, looking up, you can appreciate its true grandeur, its imposing magnitude.

This is God: His immensity, His love, and His glory are only perceived when you draw close to Him. From a distance, His greatness may seem abstract or distant; but as you draw closer, you discover the astonishing reality of His being.

God is so great that He offers you abundance, peace, love, forgiveness, and mercy. His love for you is unconditional, and His forgiveness knows no bounds. He understands that sin—whether anger, criticism, hatred, or any other form of alienation—is a force of the devil seeking to enslave you. But Jesus doesn't expect you to be perfect to draw near to Him. On the contrary, He calls you just as you are, with all your burdens and mistakes, to transform your heart and set you free. As a popular reflection says: "You don't get clean to take a bath; you take a bath to get clean."

Likewise, you don't need to be free from sin to approach Jesus; it is by being with Him that your soul is cleansed, your life is renewed, and the chains that bind you are broken. Jesus put it this way: "Come to me, all you who are weary and burdened, and I will give you rest. Take my yoke upon you and learn from me, for I am gentle and humble in heart, and you will find rest for your souls. For my yoke is easy and my burden is light" (Matthew 11:28-30). And also: "Cast all your anxiety on him because he cares for you" (1 Peter 5:7).

God doesn't just cleanse you; He transforms you and gives you an eternal purpose. His love and power can change your life forever.

FREEDOM AND ETERNAL LIFE

Sin enslaves us. It drags us into guilt, sadness, and ultimately spiritual death. But Jesus, with his sacrifice, freed us and offered us the greatest gift: eternal life.

Romans 6:22-23: "But now that you have been set free from sin and have become slaves to God, your fruit leads to holiness and the end is eternal life. For the wages of sin is death, but the gift of God is eternal life in Christ Jesus our Lord."

A CALL TO TRANSFORMATION

God calls you to approach without fear or shame. No matter how far you've fallen or how many mistakes you've made, His invitation is always open. He longs to embrace you, like the father embraced the prodigal son.

By accepting His love and mercy, you will experience a profound transformation, like that of Paul, who went from persecutor to apostle. His presence will fill you with a peace that doesn't depend on circumstances, a love that never fades, and a strength that will enable you to overcome any adversity, like David facing Goliath.

ALLOW THE GREATNESS OF GOD
TO BE REVEALED IN YOUR LIFE.

Approach Him in prayer, immerse yourself in His Word, and allow His love to transform your heart. He will break your chains, restore your life, and lead you to experience the true fulfillment that only His grace can offer.

CHAPTER 9

PRAYER: THE PORTAL TO DIVINITY

✝

Before you continue reading, I want to invite you to reflect on a profound question: what is the soul and how can we access it?

In the chapter "Sparks of God's Expansion," we saw that we all carry a divine spark within us, our soul. But now another question arises: How do we truly connect with that divinity within us?

Searching for definitions, I found one that seemed accurate to me: "The soul is the part of the individual that contains a divine portion, which imprints the individual personality, where imagination, feelings and reason reside (mind, emotion and will)."

Although this definition is useful, it does not teach us how to directly access the soul.

Today, most of us live trapped in a routine. We get up, go to work, go home, and go to sleep, repeating the endless cycle. We've neglected our spiritual life, disconnecting from our deeper purpose.

We move by inertia, trapped in material things, forgetting the supernatural gift that dwells within us.

If God, in his infinite power, endowed us with a divine spark when he created us in his image and likeness, doesn't it stand to reason that we can also access that gift to heal, restore, and overcome our fears?

The answer is yes, but to achieve this, we need to wake up. It's like in the movie *The Matrix*: do we want to remain in the illusion or do we want to wake up to the truth?

The human definition of the soul, though valuable, is not enough. Why not ask our soul directly who we are? Our soul, connected to God, possesses the wisdom we need. Let us remember: the soul existed before the body and will exist after it. It is eternal, as Scripture teaches us:

> Jeremiah 1:5: "Before I formed you in the womb I knew you, before you were born I set you apart."

> John 17:24: "the glory you have given me because you loved me before the creation of the world."

So shouldn't we listen to that inner voice before any human logic?

THE SOUL: THE TRUE DRIVER

Imagine you buy a car. You sit behind the wheel and drive it to different places. Then someone approaches the car and asks, "Who are you?" To which the car would reply, "I am a vehicle that moves on wheels." But if that same person asks you, the driver, "Who are you?" your answer will be different. You won't say, "I am a car," but rather, "I am a person who uses this car to reach my destination."

The soul works the same way. At birth, our soul enters the human body like a driver taking control of a vehicle to travel its path and fulfill the divine purpose for which it was sent.

The body is the means, but the soul defines the course and gives meaning to the journey. That's why it's essential to take care of both the body, our vehicle, and the soul, the true driver, so we can reach that final destination: the purpose for which we were created.

The problem arises when we forget that we are drivers. The body continues to function, but on autopilot. Without an awakened soul, life becomes empty, chaotic, and vulnerable to darkness.

When we lose connection with our soul, we feel empty, confused, and disoriented. To find ourselves again, we must reconnect with our Creator.

HOW DO WE ACCESS OUR SOUL?

It's like when you stand in front of a painting and try to decipher its meaning. At first glance, you only see colors, shapes, and strokes, but you don't know the true message of the work. You can speculate about its meaning, but you'll never know its true purpose until you speak to the artist and ask, "Why did you create this work? What did you want to express with it?"

Likewise, we will not understand our purpose until we speak to the One who created us.

Accessing our essence requires silencing the noise of the world. Only in the silence of the heart can we hear the voice of God.

There are two main ways to disconnect from the outside world: sleep and prayer or meditation.

Sleep unconsciously disconnects us, but prayer and meditation allow us to consciously connect with our souls.

When we pray deeply:

- We silence scattered thoughts.

- We leave distractions behind.

- We access our pure consciousness.

Only there, in love and peace, can we hear the voice of God.

As 1 John 4:8 says: "Whoever does not love does not know God, because God is love." Love is the key that opens the door to communion with our Creator.

Although our physical eyes cannot see this connection, it is as real as the air we breathe. Invisible, yet vital.

THE HOLY SPIRIT: OUR SURE GUIDE

Once in a state of deep prayer, it is essential to invoke the Holy Spirit. He protects us from deception and connects us directly to God. We can ask him:

- "Lord Jesus, who am I?"

- "What is my purpose?"

- "What truth should I embrace?"

The answers may come as visions, intuitions, inner words, or signs in everyday life.

The key is patience. Learning to listen to God is like learning a new language: it requires practice, inner silence, and perseverance.

GOD DOES NOT FAIL

When we suffer, it's easy to ask, "Why is this happening to me?" However, every difficulty can be an opportunity to draw closer to Him.

God doesn't want us to live in confusion or perpetual pain. He offers us His love and unwavering peace. As Jesus says in Matthew 16:24-26:

> "Whoever wants to be my disciple must deny themselves and take up their cross and follow me. For whoever wants to save their life will lose it, but whoever loses their life for me will find it. What good will it be for someone to gain the whole world, yet forfeit their soul? Or what can anyone give in exchange for their soul?"

Only by surrendering to Him can we find fulfillment and true purpose.

HOW TO FACILITATE
CONNECTION WITH GOD

To connect more easily with God during prayer:

- **Close your eyes:** reduce external stimuli.

- **Look for darkness or a quiet environment:** darkness encourages calm.

- **Breathe deeply:** enter into cardiac coherence, harmonizing body and mind.

- **Call upon the Holy Spirit:** "Holy Spirit, in the name of Jesus, come to me."

Upon reaching this state, we will experience an inexplicable peace, a feeling of enveloping love that transforms our inner selves. Many also find it helpful to accompany this moment with praise music, which uplifts the spirit and strengthens our connection with God.

Some spiritual practices speak of aligning the body's energy centers as a means to achieving harmony. However, in my experience, I discovered that when the Holy Spirit manifests, His power acts instantly, filling our entire being with an indescribable peace. There is no need to rely on complex techniques or long hours of meditation, because His grace transforms us in a single instant.

I remember a moment in my life when I felt His presence overwhelmingly. It was like a vibrant energy coursing through my entire body, a love so immense and inexplicable that it dissipated all my fears and worries. From that day on, the Holy Spirit began to teach me the lies I had believed and showed me the truth.

I understood that true harmony does not come from human techniques or personal efforts, but from total surrender to God and His Spirit.

God always speaks to us, but it is we who must learn to listen. As Job 33:14-18 says:

> "For God does speak—now one way, now another—though no one perceives it. In a dream, in a vision of the night, when deep sleep falls on people as they slumber in their beds, he may speak in their ears and terrify them with warnings, to turn them from wrongdoing and keep them from pride, to preserve them from the pit, their lives from perishing by the sword."

CHAPTER 10

THE PATH TO ETERNAL LOVE

In the Gospel of Matthew 19, 16-19, we read:

> "Just then a man came up to Jesus and asked, 'Teacher, what good thing must I do to get eternal life?' 'Why do you ask me about what is good?' Jesus replied. 'There is only One who is good. If you want to enter life, keep the commandments.' 'Which ones?' he inquired.

> "Jesus replied, 'You shall not murder, you shall not commit adultery, you shall not steal, you shall not give false testimony, honor your father and mother, and love your neighbor as yourself.'"

Later, in Matthew 22:34-40, Jesus summarizes the entire law in two great commandments:

> "Hearing that Jesus had silenced the Sadducees, the

Pharisees got together. One of them, an expert in the law, tested him with this question: 'Teacher, which is the greatest commandment in the Law?' Jesus replied: '"Love the Lord your God with all your heart and with all your soul and with all your mind." This is the first and greatest commandment. And the second is like it: "Love your neighbor as yourself." All the Law and the Prophets hang on these two commandments.'"

Here Jesus makes it clear that the basis of the entire law is love: first toward God, and then toward one's neighbor.

WHO IS GOD THE FATHER?

When Jesus commands us to love God, a fundamental question arises: Who is God the Father really?

Scripture reveals its essence to us in three central truths:

1. God is the source of all goodness

Jesus makes it clear that absolute goodness comes only from God. His response "There is only One who is good(…)" is given from his humanity, as the young man calls him "master" and does not yet recognize him as the Son of God.

2. God is spirit

In John 4:24, we read: "God is spirit, and his worshipers must worship in the Spirit and in truth."

This passage reminds us that God is not a material entity, but rather reminds us that our connection with Him must be internal and authentic, not merely ritualistic or external.

3. God is love

Finally, in 1 John 4:7-8, we find an essential statement: "Dear friends, let us love one another, for love comes from God. Everyone who loves has been born of God and knows God. Whoever does not love does not know God, because God is love."

God not only possesses love: He is Love in its purest form.

HOW TO TRULY WORSHIP GOD?

These passages teach us that:

- Worshipping God means living in love.

- It is necessary to deepen our spirituality, cultivating prayer, meditation and inner life.

- To direct our actions toward good is to reflect His goodness in the world.

We cannot worship Him only with external practices, but with a transformed spirit that is in tune with His essence.

JESUS: THE SON WHO REVEALS THE FATHER

Jesus claimed to be the Son of God, but many disbelieved, just as someone who presents his identity and is still questioned. However, Jesus backed up his claim with miracles. He healed, delivered, raised the dead, and finally, conquered death by resurrecting himself on the third day. He didn't just speak of God's love; he embodied it.

PERFECT LOVE ELIMINATES FEAR

1 John 4:18 states: "There is no fear in love. But perfect love drives out fear, because fear has to do with punishment. The one who fears is not made perfect in love."

Fear does not come from God. It is the devil who sows fear, worry, and anguish to distance us from divine peace. When we live in God's love, fear loses its power.

To remain in this life of love and freedom, Jesus invites us to:

- Pray constantly, to strengthen our connection with the Father.

- Participate in the Eucharist, receiving the life of Christ within us.

- To love one's neighbor, thus reflecting divine love in the world.

ETERNAL LIFE BEGINS TODAY

Eternal life is not just a future reward: it begins here and now, when we live connected to God's love.

Jesus calls us to be light in the midst of darkness, to reflect his love in our words and actions. As Matthew 5:14-16 reminds us: "You are the light of the world… Let your light so shine before men, that they may see your good works and glorify your Father who is in heaven."

Every small act of love and kindness we perform is a spark of the eternal life that already dwells within us.

● ● ●

God calls us to live a life free from fear and full of love.

As we cultivate this connection with Him—through prayer, fellowship, and service to others—we become living witnesses of His goodness, His spirit, and His love.

May our life be a reflection of that light that never goes out, so that, at the end of our journey, we may hear from His mouth:

> "Well done, good and faithful servant! (…) Come and
> share your master's happiness!" (Matthew 25:21).

CHAPTER 11

THE PATH TO OUR ORIGINAL IDENTITY

✝

In the previous chapters, we've talked about our connection to God, the divine spark that dwells within the soul, and the transformative power of communion and the Holy Spirit. Now, in this reflection, I want to take you a step further: to discover that we are not only connected to God, but that we were created in His image and likeness, called to live from that original identity. This is a profound call to remember who we are in essence and to live according to that spiritual truth we carry within.

Jesus is the incarnation of God through the Holy Spirit, the living manifestation of divine energy. Therefore, he possessed the divine power that enabled him to perform miracles and extraordinary actions. Jesus is God not only because of the works he performed, but also because of the love and peace he radiated, a state that any human being can achieve.

In his infinite wisdom, Jesus sent us the Holy Spirit, who gives us the strength to overcome our human concerns and live in harmony, just as we were originally created to do. The same Holy Spirit that was in Jesus is the one we now receive through baptism.

Jesus showed us that he was not tied to earthly worries like money, family conflicts, or daily responsibilities. His life was an example of total trust in God, stripping himself of material things and living in spiritual fullness. Although these worries seem inevitable to us, the Holy Spirit offers us the power to face them with faith and serenity, drawing us closer to the love and peace that Jesus lived.

It is thanks to the Holy Spirit that we can aspire to be like Jesus: to live in peace, to love without measure, and to find fulfillment in our relationship with God and our loved ones here on Earth.

What a great joy and blessing is this gift that God has given us!

OUR TRUE IDENTITY

If we analyze the following syllogism:

> Premise 1: God is Divine Love.
>
> Premise 2: Jesus is Divine Love.
>
> Conclusion: Jesus is God.

Following this logic, a key question arises: If we manage to be divine love, wouldn't we also be getting closer to our divine nature? The answer is found in Genesis 1:26-27:

> "Then God said, 'Let us make mankind in our image, in our likeness' (…) So God created mankind in his own image, in the image of God he created them; male and female he created them."

This confirms that we were created in the image and likeness of God, which means that we carry divine love as our original essence. Our soul is destined to unite with Him because we are part of the body of Christ.

This is how St. Paul explains it in 1 Corinthians 12:12-14, 27: "Just as a body, though one, has many parts, but all its many parts form one body, so it is with Christ. For we were all baptized by one Spirit so as to form one body (...) you are the body of Christ, and each one of you is a part of it."

It is as if the scattered water droplets—mentioned in the chapter "The Divine Connection: Sparks of God's Expansion"—return to their source: the eternal source from which they were separated.

THE BIG DECISION

The great challenge is to decide how we want to live:

Will we accept our original identity, as beings created in the image and likeness of God? Or will we prefer the lie of sin, which defines us as unworthy and separates us from our essence?

Remember: our actions build our identity. If we recognize Jesus as our God and act like Him, we can return to our true nature: a life of holiness, peace, and authentic love.

This is the divine purpose that awaits us, but the final decision is in our hands.

THE CALL
TO HOLINESS

I've been reflecting on the Lord's Prayer, the prayer Jesus taught us. As I analyzed it carefully, a connection emerged that led me to interpret it from a different perspective than the traditional one. Perhaps some scholars disagree with this view, but I wish to share it, with humility and openness, as a way to delve deeper into its meaning.

The prayer begins like this:

"Our Father, who art in heaven, hallowed be thy name…"

The phrase "hallowed be thy name" is meant literally: that God's name should be hallowed. However, I stopped and asked myself: "How can we sanctify someone who is already a saint?"

In Leviticus 11:44, God Himself says: "I am the Lord your God; *consecrate yourselves and be holy, because I am holy.*"

I understand expressions like "Praise your name" or "Holy are you, Lord Jesus," because they acknowledge God's holiness. But "hallowing his name" raised a concern in me: if God is already holy, what are we really asking for?

THE NAME OF GOD AND ITS MEANING

To find a possible answer, I went to the origin of God's name. In Exodus 3:13-15, God reveals it to Moses.

> "Then Moses said to God, 'If I come to the people of Israel and say to them, "The God of your fathers has sent me to you," and they ask me, "What is his name?" what shall I say to them?' God said to Moses:

> "Ehyeh Asher Ehyeh" (I Am Who I Am). And he said: "Say this to the people of Israel: 'Ehyeh (I Am) has sent me to you.'" God also said to Moses:

> "Say this to the people of Israel: 'YHWH, the God of your fathers, the God of Abraham, the God of Isaac, and the God of Jacob, has sent me to you. This is my name forever, and by this name I will be remembered from generation to generation.'"

The name YHWH comes from the Hebrew root *hayah*, which means "being." That is, God identifies himself as the *Being self.*

THE NAME OF GOD IN THE LORD'S PRAYER

If we replace the name with what it represents, we could read: "Our Father, who art in heaven, hallowed be thy being…"

This reformulation offers an interesting interpretation. In Romans 12:4-5, Saint Paul speaks of how we are part of the body of Christ, that is, of the Being of God: "For just as each of us has one body with many members, and these members do not all have the same function, *so in Christ we,* though many, form one body."

"*Now you are the body of Christ,* and each one of you is a part of it." (1 Corinthians 12:27)

"*For we are members of his body,* of his flesh and of his bones." (Ephesians 5:30)

So, if we are part of the Being of Christ—who is God—and we say "hallowed be thy Being," could it not mean that we are asking for ourselves, the baptized, to be sanctified, since we are a living part of Him?

Jesus is God, and every word He spoke was chosen with divine intention. He didn't say "Hallowed is your name," as if we were merely acknowledging His holiness. Instead, He said "Hallowed be your name," which *implies a request — a desire for something to happen.*

We know that Jesus often spoke in parables and messages filled with spiritual depth, leaving clues for those with ears to hear. From this perspective, it could be understood that Jesus was asking for His holiness to be manifested in us, the children of God. Because if we are part of His Being — as He Himself identified when He said "I Am" — then asking that His name "be hallowed" is, at its core, a plea *for us to be sanctified in Him.*

THE LORD'S PRAYER AS A PROCESS OF SANCTIFICATION

If we continue reading the structure of the prayer, we notice that each petition seems to lead us to holiness:

- Thy Kingdom come (a Holy Kingdom)

- Thy will be done (living according to His will sanctifies us)

- Give us our daily bread (Jesus, the Bread of Life)

- Forgive our offenses (spiritual cleansing)

- Lead us not into temptation (protection from evil)

Everything points to a process of inner transformation to sanctified us. From this perspective, prayer could be understood as a request to be sanctified, since God *already is eternally sanctified.*

"But just as he who called you is holy, so be holy in all you do; for it is written: *'Be holy, because I am holy'.*" (1 Peter 1:15-16)

"For he chose us in him before the creation of the world *to be holy* and blameless in his sight." (Ephesians 1:4)

A NEW PERSPECTIVE, THE SAME MESSAGE

This interpretation does not alter the content of the Lord's Prayer, but rather invites us to view it from a new perspective. God does not need to be sanctified; his name is already holy. But we, as his children, bear that name within us. Asking that "his name be hallowed" may, at its core, be a plea for his holiness to be reflected in us as well, who are members of his body, a living part of his Being.

As Jesus said:

"Whoever has ears to hear, let them hear."

CHAPTER 13

FASTING: AN ACT OF LOVE AND CONNECTION WITH GOD

L et's imagine the Christmas season is approaching, a time filled with traditions, gatherings, and gestures of affection. It's common for families to gather to share and, often, exchange gifts. As parents, we don't expect our children to give us anything material. What we truly value is their company, the time we share, and the meaningful moments we build together.

If one of them decides to give us a gift, of course we receive it with joy and gratitude. But our love for the other children who didn't bring anything doesn't diminish in the least. We know that love doesn't depend on a gift, because the most valuable thing is the relationship we have with them.

This analogy helps us better understand the spiritual meaning of fasting. Fasting means voluntarily giving up something—food, drink, or pleasure—for the purpose of focusing our attention on God and strengthening our spiritual life.

We know that God's love for us doesn't depend on whether we fast or not. His love is perfect, unconditional, and eternal. When we fast sincerely, we do so as a gesture of gratitude, humility, or intercession, demonstrating our desire to draw closer to Him.

Fasting is not a burden or an obligation. It is a voluntary expression of love. God is not offended if we do not practice it, but He is pleased when we do so with a willing heart. Through fasting, we acknowledge our dependence on His grace and remember that everything we are and have comes from Him.

Furthermore, at the end of the fast, we appreciate even more his provision: not only physical, but also spiritual.

THE POWER OF FASTING AND PRAYER

Throughout Scripture, we find numerous passages that link prayer and fasting as a powerful way to connect with God. Here are some key examples:

> "While they were worshiping the Lord and fasting, the Holy Spirit said, 'Set apart for me Barnabas and Saul for the work to which I have called them.' So after *they had fasted and prayed*, they placed their hands on them and sent them off." (Acts 13:2-3)

> "...*with prayer and fasting*, committed them to the Lord, in whom they had put their trust." (Acts 14:23)

> "This kind of demons can only come out with *prayer and fasting*." (Mark 9:29)

This leads us to ask: Why do prayer and fasting go hand in hand?

1. Prayer: Our Connection to God

- It brings us closer to His presence and strengthens our faith.

- It aligns us with His will, beyond our desires.

- It calls upon His power to act in difficult or impossible situations.

3. Fasting: a discipline that liberates

- It is an act of humility, where we recognize our fragility and dependence on God.

- It helps us eliminate distractions and focus our hearts on the eternal.

- It purifies the spirit, sensitizing it to hear the voice of God more clearly.

A COMPARISON TO UNDERSTAND IT BETTER

Imagine you're going to play a football game and, an hour beforehand, you decide to eat a rib-eye steak with dessert. How would you feel on the field? Slow, heavy, maybe uncomfortable.

Now transfer this image to the spiritual plane. When we desire a deep connection with God, fasting acts as a preparation: it clears the body, quiets the soul, and frees up inner space to hear His voice clearly.

FASTING AS A SPIRITUAL TOOL

Ultimately, fasting isn't a requirement for God to love us more. We already have His love.

It is a tool that helps us free ourselves from noise, organize our priorities, and sensitize our spirit to receive His direction, peace, and strength.

When combined with prayer, fasting becomes a powerful channel of communion with God.

God doesn't expect a perfect sacrifice. He only expects a sincere heart.

CHAPTER 14

THE QUEEN ON
THE DIVINE BOARD

✝

I heard this little reflection from a priest and I want to share it.

Chess lovers know that, of all the pieces on the board, the king is the center of everything. It is the most important piece, the one that must be protected at all costs, because without it the game is lost. Next to the king, we find the second most powerful piece: the queen. Although not the most important, it is undoubtedly the most versatile, with the ability to move freely in any direction, fulfilling essential tasks to protect and advance on behalf of the king. It is an indispensable piece for your strategy and success.

Likewise, the Immaculate Virgin Mary is present in Jesus's divine work. She does not occupy the place of the King; that place belongs solely to Jesus, our Savior and Lord. However, the Virgin Mary is a key figure in God's mission. She moves with grace and power wherever necessary, doing the work the King entrusts to her, guiding us, interceding for us, and fulfilling an essential role in the divine plan.

Just as in chess, where the queen plays a crucial role in supporting the king, Mary is indispensable in the Church. She does not replace Jesus, but works in perfect harmony with Him. This is why so many of the faithful pray to the Virgin Mary, not as an end in itself, but as a path to God. We know that her maternal love always leads us to Jesus, and that, like a loving mother, she intercedes for us and helps us in our greatest need.

In chess, the queen fights, protects, and sacrifices if necessary to fulfill her purpose. In the same way, Mary has dedicated her life to the service of God. She is our guide on the chessboard of life, leading us with wisdom and love toward the King. Just as a game without the queen is harder to win, a spiritual life without the help of the Virgin is a more arduous path.

Therefore, we ask her to come to us, to intercede and help us, always in accordance with God's will. Mary is the perfect example of humility and obedience to the Lord, and by trusting in her, we follow her example: to live not for our own glory, but for the glory of the King.

SATAN, KING OF LIES

THE BIG LIE: THE DISTORTION
OF THE TRUTH OF OUR IDENTITY.

Why do we do evil? What drives us to fight, steal, start wars, argue with our loved ones, or react angrily toward strangers? What prevents us from constantly living in a state of peace?

Psychology teaches us that our emotional wounds, accumulated throughout life, shape our behavior. We learn by observing and repeating behaviors. As the saying goes, "Monkey see, monkey do." However, to understand the real origin of evil, we must go back beyond our personal or family experiences to the beginning of humanity.

If we were created for good, how did evil get into our nature? The answer lies at the origin of the big lie.

According to the Genesis story, Satan deceived Adam and Eve into believing they would be like God by eating from the forbidden tree. What he didn't tell them was that they were already like God, having been created in His image and likeness. This was the first great lie: making them doubt their identity.

From that moment on, humankind was trapped in a distortion of its true being. Satan sowed doubt, insecurity, and fear, and so wounds began to multiply, deforming human nature, distancing us from love, and sowing pain and evil in the world.

Throughout the centuries, Satan and his army have continued to attack our minds and hearts, keeping us from God's purpose. This is why the Old Testament depicts so many wars, cruelties, and disorders: humanity, disconnected from its divine identity, was manipulated into living under deception.

BARRIERS THAT SEPARATE US FROM GOD

Every wound we receive, every fear, every worry and anger build barriers that distance us from God.

Where there is fear, there is no love. And where there is no love, God cannot dwell, for God is love (1 John 4:8). And how can we hear His voice if our souls are covered by layers of lies and deception?

The first and most serious lie Satan planted was to make us doubt our identity as children of God. From there all the other wounds arose, each one building a new wall between us and our Creator.

Today, Satan continues to attack our identity, but now he does so on the physical plane as well. His next step is to distort our human identity. The idea that one can choose one's identity, that one is born male but can become female, or even identify as an animal or another gender, is a new strategy to plunge us into chaos. When a human being loses their identity in both soul and body, they feel lost, without direction or purpose. This is Satan's goal: to destroy us at our roots, separating us even further from God and the truth of who we are.

Scarcity, anxiety, and constant worry are not part of God's plan for us. God created us to live in fullness and love. But the devil works day and night to convince us otherwise.

It's time to break down barriers and recognize the truth: we are children of God, created in His image, called to live in His love and truth. Only by recovering our identity can we live freely in the peace and fulfillment God designed for us.

THE CONSEQUENCE OF THE WOUND

Every emotional wound leaves a lie planted in our hearts.

I share with you two personal examples:

- When I was robbed in my company, I suffered a financial and family crisis. From that experience arose the lie that I was a fool for not foreseeing it.

- As a child, I experienced rejection, which implanted the lie that I was not valued.

These wounds, although they were external circumstances, sowed false beliefs about my worth and my identity.

We all carry similar wounds within us. But *there is a way to break through those lies and heal*: the powerful name of Jesus.

HOW TO BREAK THE
LIES AND HEAL THE SOUL

To heal wounds and erase lies, forgiveness is essential. This must be done *in the name of Jesus*, because Satan and evil spirits cannot remain where Jesus is. Furthermore, it must *be done out loud*, since the devil cannot read our thoughts; he needs to hear us, just as Jesus cast out demons with verbal authority.

It's like when someone pulls on your arm: if you only think, "Let me go," that person won't listen. The same thing happens with the devil, but on the level of the soul. He doesn't respond to thoughts, but to authority spoken out loud. When you say, "In the name of Jesus, let me go," you are exercising your identity as a child of God. The devil obeys you because the Holy Spirit who dwelt in Jesus also dwells in you.

When you are in a state of connection with Jesus and the Holy Spirit, you can follow this process:

1. Identify sins and ask for forgiveness.

Say in prayer:

"Lord Jesus, show me the sins I have committed."

Whatever comes to your mind, confess it by saying: "Lord Jesus, forgive me for [mention the sin] that I committed against [person] and against You."

2. Ask Jesus who it is you need to forgive.

Say in prayer:

"Lord Jesus, show me the people I need to forgive."

Remember: the first names or images that come to mind are clear signals. If you want to go into more detail, just ask.

"Jesus, show me what experience of mine (dad, brother, mom, friend, etc.) hurt me"

3. Declare forgiveness out loud.

For each person or experience, say:

> *"In the powerful name of Jesus, I choose to forgive [name and/ or experience] for [the harm they caused you]. "*

4. Reject the hurt out loud.

Identify the wound that experience left you, for example, abandonment, contempt, or anger. Ask:

> *"Lord Jesus, show me the wounds that are implanted in me."*

When you receive answers say:

> *"In the name of Jesus, I reject the wound of [abandonment, rejection, anger...] that [name or situation] left me. I surrender this wound to the foot of Jesus' cross and command that it never return to me again."*

5. Eliminate the lie and replace it with the truth.

Question in prayer:

> *"Lord Jesus, what lie did the enemy plant through that wound?"*

Once the lie is identified, proclaim:

> *"Holy Spirit, in the name of Jesus, I reject the lie that [for example: I am worthless]. Fill me with your truth, your love, peace, and appreciation. "*

> **Note:** The devil not only implants emotional lies, but also lies of knowledge that distort God's truth. Many false doctrines or "spiritual" practices stem from this deception.

Therefore, it is vital to discern with the Holy Spirit and remain firm in the teachings of the Word.

6. Seal the healing

Close your prayer by saying:

"In the name of Jesus, I bless every word that comes from God to me, so that it may bear fruit in my life. And I reject every word that does not come from Him, so that it has no power over me."

REMINDER: GOD FORGETS OUR SINS

When we sincerely confess our sins, God not only forgives us, but also forgets. But sometimes we continue to carry guilt that has already been absolved. This constant remorse comes not from God, but from the enemy, who seeks to keep us trapped in the past to distance us from the present, where God dwells. This is poignantly illustrated in a story by Saint Faustina Kowalska.

She had a vision of Jesus, and a priest asked her, if he really was Jesus, to ask him what her last confessed sins were. When Faustina did so, Jesus replied:

"I don't remember."

That's the power of divine forgiveness: God doesn't keep records. If He forgets, why shouldn't you?

Jesus came to set you free. His forgiveness not only cleanses your soul, but also restores your identity as a child of God.

When you confess sincerely, you are reunited with Christ and regain your holiness. So make this truth yours:

In forgiveness, we are renewed. In Jesus, we are holy.

• • •

Genesis 3:1-6 recounts the fall of man:

> Now the serpent was more crafty than any of the wild
> animals the Lord God had made. He said to the woman,
> "Did God really say, 'You must not eat from any tree in
> the garden'?"
>
> The woman said to the serpent, "We may eat fruit from
> the trees in the garden, but God did say, 'You must not
> eat fruit from the tree that is in the middle of the garden,
> and you must not touch it, or you will die.'"
>
> "You will not certainly die," the serpent said to the woman.
> "For God knows that when you eat from it your eyes will be
> opened, and you will be like God, knowing good and evil."
>
> When the woman saw that the fruit of the tree was good
> for food and pleasing to the eye, and also desirable for
> gaining wisdom, she took some and ate it. She also gave
> some to her husband, who was with her, and he ate it.

Thus began the great spiritual battle in which we are still engaged.

CHAPTER 16

BREAKING THE CHAINS OF THE SOUL

For this reflection, I want to invite you to put on a special pair of glasses. Not ones that see your physical body... but your soul.

Imagine your day is starting. You're on your way to work, and suddenly a car cuts you off. You react angrily, honk, and raise your hand. You arrive at the office, and your boss yells at you:

"Get it right! You always leave things half-done!"

Annoyed, you return home. Your children are fighting during dinner, and you yell at them:

"Stop fighting!"

One answers you angrily:

"You're the worst dad in the world!"

Then you argue with your wife.

So the day progresses, between insults you give… and insults you receive.

Now look at it from the spiritual plane.

Your soul began the day cleansed and free. But every time you cause harm, the enemy throws a chain that hooks onto your left hand. And every time you're hurt, another chain attaches to your right hand.

You offend: left chain. You were hurt: right chain.

And so, little by little, those chains accumulate, straining your soul and stretching it until it's exhausted. Even though you continue to live your daily routine, inside you are tired, oppressed, chained.

If you do nothing, your soul will begin to weaken. Addictions, sadness, anxiety, insomnia, or even illnesses will appear.

As Catholics, we know how to free ourselves from the left side: we confess, we ask for forgiveness, and God breaks those chains.

But… what about the right side?

Have you ever confessed about the injuries you received?

Lack of forgiveness toward those who hurt us keeps those chains intact. If we don't heal those wounds, the devil continues to oppress, drag, and tear at our soul.

ONLY FORGIVENESS CAN BREAK THOSE CHAINS.

Many people go to a psychologist, and that can help. But there are wounds that only Jesus can heal, because the one who holds those chains is not human, but spiritual. It is the devil who pulls the chains, and no human being, no matter how well prepared, can break those chains without the intervention of Christ.

HOW DO THEY BREAK?

The answer is in Luke 4:18-19:

"The Spirit of the Lord is on me, because he has anointed me to proclaim good news to the poor. He has sent me to proclaim freedom for the prisoners and recovery of sight for the blind, to set the oppressed free, to proclaim the year of the Lord's favor."

Jesus came to set you free. The method is simple, yet powerful. In a state of grace and communion with God, firmly say: "In the name of Jesus, I choose to forgive [name of person] for [name the harm]."

That's all.

You don't need to feel forgiveness.

Forgiveness is a decision, not a feeling.

And that decision, made in the name of Jesus, breaks the soul chains that hold you in resentment, guilt, or bitterness.

Do it daily.

Memory is fragile. Sometimes we forget what we caused or what was done to us, but the chains remain, silently oppressing the soul. That's why it's so important to maintain a daily practice of forgiveness: so that no chains remain hidden, oppressing our soul.

LIES THAT PREVENT FORGIVENESS

The enemy knows this. That's why he sows thoughts like:

1. Forgiveness is allowing myself to be hurt again.

2. Forgiveness is justifying what was done to me.

3. Forgiveness means reconciling with the aggressor.

4. Forgiveness requires that you feel it.

5. To forgive is to forget the emotional debt.

They are all lies.

Forgiveness is a spiritual key that frees your soul.

When you don't forgive or ask for forgiveness, you give authority to the enemy. God gave us dominion in the beginning: "So God created man in his own image [...] and said to them, '*fill the earth and subdue it*'" (Genesis 1:27-28).

By sinning, we hand over that authority to the devil. That's why, in the temptation of Jesus, the enemy says: "All authority has been given to me" (Matthew 28:18).

Who gave it to him? We did, by not forgiving.

Thanks to Jesus, we can get it back.

He came to:

- Break chains.

- Give you back your freedom.

- Restore your identity.

- Reconnect your soul with the Father.

When you forgive in the name of Jesus, his power acts. Your soul is lightened, and you experience freedom, healing, and peace. "Forgiveness doesn't change the past, but it can transform your future."

Today is the day to let go of what binds you.

You don't have to wait to feel ready, or wait for everything to be in order. God doesn't ask for perfection, just a willing heart. In the name of Jesus, you can begin to heal, forgive, and regain your true freedom.

Don't live chained by the wounds of the past any longer. Jesus already paid the price.

You just have to take the key He gave you... and *open the door to your liberation.*

"*So if the Son sets you free, you will be free indeed.*" (John 8:36)

CHAPTER 17

SPIRITUAL DECEPTION

✝

Today, there is a great deal of confusion and misunderstanding regarding people who call themselves "mediums" or who claim to communicate with angels. It's increasingly common to hear about acquaintances seeking out these individuals in the hopes of speaking with a deceased relative or receiving messages from supposed "angels of light." And while I understand the longing behind this search— who wouldn't want to hear the voice of a departed loved one?—we must be alert, because what appear to be comforting answers may, in fact, be spiritual traps.

The first thing we must understand is that these "angels" or "familiars" with whom mediums claim to communicate are not who they claim to be. They are, in fact, demonic entities disguised to deceive and lead people away from God.

Some might argue: "He told me things that only my relative and I knew. He called me by my childhood nickname, told a story no one else knew, and even imitated the voice and way of speaking." And yes, it's possible the entity did so with chilling precision. But there's an explanation for this: demons have been present in the spiritual realm since your birth. They observe every detail of your life, analyze you deeply, and know how to deceive you.

Satan is the father of lies (John 8:44), and his demons aim to draw souls away from God. They know what you most want to hear, and they say it to trap you, feeding your curiosity and the temptation to continue exploring the hidden. But behind this apparent comfort, their true goal is to open a door to their influence, leading you away from the light of God and leading you to place your trust in forces that do not come from Him.

THE MOST OBVIOUS SIGN:
SPIRITUAL COMMERCE

One of the clearest signs that these practices do not come from God is that they charge money for them, and the decisive criterion is the fruit of the message. When the Holy Spirit speaks, He does so to set you free and heal your soul; by contrast, mediums, psychics, and channelers may share intimate truths, but without fruit—they profit from people's faith by offering "messages from beyond" in exchange for large sums of money.

This is where we must ask ourselves: Did Jesus charge for healing, prophesying, or liberating the oppressed?

Of course not! Jesus, who is the Son of God and the ultimate expression of divine love, never asked for anything in return when he performed miracles. On the contrary, he left a clear instruction to his disciples in Matthew 10:8: "Heal the sick, raise the dead, cleanse those who have leprosy, drive out demons. *Freely you have received; freely give.*"

God's power is not a marketable commodity. His gifts are free and should be used for edification, not enrichment. This is in stark contrast to mediums, who make a lucrative business out of spirituality.

THE DIRECT RELATIONSHIP WITH GOD

Another big lie the enemy has spread is the idea that we need intermediaries to communicate with God. But the reality is that, as children of God, we have direct access to Him. We don't need anyone for guidance. God speaks to us directly through prayer, the Bible, and the Holy Spirit.

However, we must be aware that even when we seek God, the enemy will try to infiltrate our communication. How can we know whether a message is from God or not?

A message from God will always edify, encourage, and comfort. As 1 Corinthians 14:3 says: "But the one who prophesies speaks to people for their strengthening, encouraging and comfort."

On the contrary, if the message you receive causes you fear, anguish, anxiety, despair, or any negative emotion, it does not come from God, but from an evil spirit seeking to disturb you.

ENERGY MANIPULATION AND DECEPTIVE SPIRITUAL PRACTICES

The devil, although a fallen angel, possesses profound knowledge of the energies created by God. And although he has no power over the Creator, he can manipulate the creation, diverting them toward seemingly harmless practices that can actually open doors to evil influences.

Some of these practices include:

- Reiki
- Energy crystals
- Salts and candles to attract "good vibes"
- Tarot and astrology
- The philosophies of Buddhism and Hinduism focused on energies and vibrations

Although many believe these practices are simply tools for well-being or "positive energy," they can actually become channels for spiritual manipulation. Satan is cunning and often presents himself not as something dark and obvious, but as an "angel of light" to deceive the unwary. As 2 Corinthians 11:14 says, "And no wonder, for Satan himself masquerades as an angel of light."

Sometimes, the people offering these practices seem to have good intentions: perhaps they have a friendly appearance, speak of love and well-being, or even decorate their space with images of angels and saints. But this is no guarantee that they are acting with a heart filled with genuine love. If that person truly had so much love and desire to help, why would they charge for your care? Genuine love doesn't seek profit; it's a love that gives without expecting anything in return. If a spiritual practice is commercialized, it's a clear sign that it doesn't come from God, because He doesn't charge for the gifts He gives us.

The danger is that these practices can sow confusion and lead us away from the true path. Instead of placing our trust in God, we can be tempted to seek answers from sources other than Him.

THE ONLY TRUTH: JESUS CHRIST

In the face of all this spiritual distortion, the only immutable truth is Jesus Christ. He is the only mediator between God and men, as 1

Timothy 2:5 says, "For there is one God and one mediator between God and mankind, the man Christ Jesus."

If we truly want to connect with the divine, we don't need to resort to dubious practices or people who profit from faith. We simply need to go directly to God in prayer, read His Word, and live in communion with Him.

DON'T FALL FOR THE DECEPTION

It's understandable that the desire to communicate with a deceased loved one or receive spiritual guidance may be strong. But we must remember that God is the only one who can provide true comfort and direction.

The enemy will do everything possible to deceive us, disguising his traps as light, love, and wisdom. But we must not forget that behind these attractive spiritual experiences lies a strategy to distance us from God.

If we want to know the truth and live in the light, we must remain firm in God's Word, reject any practice that does not come from Him, and always seek His presence.

Only in God do we find truth, life, and true peace.

PART 2

THE AWAKENING OF CONSCIOUSNESS

CHAPTER 18

MASTER YOUR EMOTIONS, MASTER YOUR LIFE

Master your emotions and you will
master your body and your life.

Emotions, an essential part of what makes us human, exert a profound influence on our mood, behavior, and reactions. Although they are often underestimated, they play a decisive role in our physical, mental, and spiritual health. That's why I begin this chapter with a powerful phrase: "Master your emotions, and you will master your body and your life."

To fully understand this truth, we need to delve into how emotions are generated and their impact on our well-being. Every day, we generate, on average, 60,000 thoughts. Of these, 95% are fleeting, unconscious, and based on our past experiences.

Unfortunately, as psychologist Roy Baumeister demonstrated in a 2001 study, people tend to remember negative information more easily than positive information. According to this research (Bad Is

Stronger Than Good), negative emotions have a stronger and more lasting impact on the human mind than positive experiences.

BUT WHY DOES THIS HAPPEN?

From a spiritual perspective, this is also due to the enemy's constant attacks. Although we cannot see it with our physical eyes or explain it with human logic, the devil works by sowing negative thoughts and emotions—such as fear, anger, or sadness—to weaken us. Thus, these emotions tend to stay with us and dominate us if we do not confront them consciously and with God's help.

When not managed properly, negative emotions leave a deep mark. They can become a dominant force that compromises our emotional, mental, and spiritual balance. But when we learn to recognize, manage, and surrender them to the Lord, we begin to regain control of our bodies, our decisions, and, ultimately, our entire lives.

Thought is the root of emotion. A negative thought—often inspired by the enemy—can trigger emotions such as fear, anxiety, or anger, which trigger the release of hormones such as cortisol and adrenaline, which are responsible for our feeling stress. Conversely, positive thoughts activate hormones such as oxytocin, serotonin, and dopamine, which generate well-being and peace.

When negative thoughts repeat themselves uncontrollably, they generate a kind of "emotional cascade" that affects our body and mind. The most worrying thing is that we are often unaware of these thoughts, as they repeat automatically like an echo that only reinforces the pain, offering no real solution.

So, a fundamental question arises: *Why do we remain trapped in this web of negative thoughts if we want the best for ourselves?*

The answer rests in the devil's lies and his constant attacks. If God is perfect love, his opposite is fear, deception, and confusion. The enemy knows that if he can keep us bound to fear, he will distance us from God's perfect love.

The only way to break this cycle is to identify the source of these negative thoughts and heal them from the root. That's why it's so important to ask the Holy Spirit: "Why do I feel this way? What's at the root of this emotion?"

Many times we will discover that this emotion is born from a wound from the past that has not yet been healed.

A powerful practice is meditation with Jesus. During prayer, ask Him to reveal the origin of your thoughts and emotions. He may show you memories that explain where your hurt comes from. When you identify it, name it and give it to Jesus. Then, forgive whoever caused you that hurt.

It is crucial to verbalize it: "In the name of Jesus, I choose to forgive [name] for [saying out loud what he did to you]," because the devil cannot read your mind.

This process of inner healing will make you more aware of your thoughts and prevent you from falling into constant emotional exhaustion. Otherwise, you will live under the control of the devil, tied to the wounds of the past and without the freedom to live fully.

We know it's not easy to be mindful all the time, especially if you have children. Raising them involves facing conflicts that often awaken emotions buried deep within us. The key is to recognize when we're acting reactively, stop, reflect, and make a change.

For example, when we yell at our children for disobeying us, perhaps it's not just because of the act itself, but because we feel we lack authority. Perhaps that reaction stems from a childhood wound, when we didn't feel respected or valued. Identifying that pattern, forgiving the person who made us feel that way, and surrendering that lie to the Lord frees us to act with greater awareness and love toward our children.

If we remove these wounds and the lies they left behind, it will be much easier to live from inner peace, negotiate with our children, and guide them with loving authority, not imposition. Jesus said, "He who was seated on the throne said, 'I am making everything new!'" (Revelation 21:5).

He can renew your heart if you allow Him.

Remember also that God forgives all sins and forgets them completely. Therefore, there's no reason for your mind to remain stuck in the past. Ask for forgiveness, forgive others, and move on.

A phrase my father told me when I was a child always stays with me: "If you don't act as you think, you'll end up thinking as you act." This phrase reminds me of the importance of living coherently, guided by conscious thoughts that reflect God's truth. If we aren't conscious of what we think, we lose control of how we act.

And as our faith teaches us, conscience is a sacred gift. It is the voice of God speaking to us in the depths of our soul. The Catechism of the Catholic Church says in number 1776: "His conscience is man's most secret core and his sanctuary. There he is alone with God whose voice echoes in his depths."

Prayer nourishes this awareness. In the silence of the heart, we find God. He gives us the strength to act with love, heal our wounds, and transform our lives.

CHAPTER 19

SOCIAL MEDIA AND THE EMOTIONAL IMPACT

Social media, in many ways, has been a blessing, allowing us to share our joy, success, beauty, and life with the world. However, it has also given rise to a distorted reality that often hides problems and promotes an unrealistic vision of happiness and perfection. This distorted reality has triggered a host of negative effects on society, including the rise of vice, self-centeredness, and destructive emotions such as envy, depression, and criticism.

Envy manifests when we see images of others' seemingly perfect lives on social media. Depression can arise from comparing our lives to these idealized representations. Criticism is often used to belittle others and elevate oneself.

Most of us avoid showing our weaknesses for fear of appearing vulnerable. So, we fill our social media with an edited version of reality, where everything seems fine. But this false image not only harms us, but also generates destructive emotions in others. A vicious cycle forms: I see a "perfect" image, feel inadequate, and in response, I post another "perfect" image to compensate... and someone else feels bad again.

But the truth, the one we all know but few show, is that all of us—even the genuinely happy—have gone through dark, painful moments, days when we felt like we couldn't take it anymore.

These difficult moments are what make us strong, what teach us how to grow, and what prepare us to achieve true happiness. In them we unleash that "inner drive," that fire that drives us forward.

Instead of feeding this culture of appearances, it would be valuable to see more people sharing their vulnerable moments and how they overcame them. Learning from the struggles of others is much more enriching than continuing to compare ourselves to an idealized image that isn't even real.

The misuse of social media has become one of the greatest dangers to human soul. People become hypnotized by cell phones: their minds shut down, their energy is drained, addictive chemicals are triggered, and destructive emotions appear. The cell phone takes control. Social media takes over consciousness, causing people to live on automatic, within the Matrix, far from their spirituality.

And we return to the root:

What is the main objective of the devil?

- Turn away from God.

- Move away from your soul.

- Prevent you from talking to God.

Satan is the one who fuels that cell phone addiction. He's the one who pushes you to fall into comparison, envy, and frustration. Many will say: "How exaggerated! The devil has nothing to do with this."

But I'll tell you something: everything that opposes love, everything that disconnects you from your soul, comes from the enemy who seeks to destroy you. And the misuse of social media is one of his favorite tools today.

Therefore, we need to find a conscious and healthy balance in our use of cell phones and social media.

We need to wake up, regain control, and reconnect with what really matters: our soul, our conscience, and our relationship with God.

CHAPTER 20

THE ART OF POSITIVE SPEECH

We've talked about thoughts in the chapter "Master Your Emotions, Control Your Life," I want to share something interesting about how our brain works. It's crucial to understand that our brains don't differentiate between negative and positive statements.

For example, have you ever been told, "Don't think of a pink elephant"? In that instant, in a matter of milliseconds, what happened? Yes, you thought of a pink elephant, even though you were told not to! Our minds work at an astonishing speed, processing everything they hear, and they travel at the speed of light. That's why, when someone tells us, "Don't do certain things," our minds pick up exactly what they asked us not to do. Our reasoning is what then tells us that it shouldn't be done.

That's why, in recent years, a positive approach to talking to children has been promoted, as their reasoning ability is still developing. For example, if a child is yelling, it's more effective to tell them "Keep it down" rather than "Don't yell." The reason is that their minds

109

process the word "yell," and their reasoning ability isn't yet developed enough to fully understand the negative.

This approach applies to many other lessons parents try to teach their children. For example, if a baby hits his sister, instead of saying, "Don't hit your sister," it's more effective to say, "Caress your sister." Babies lack the ability to reason, and their brains process hitting if it's communicated in a negative way. It's not that the child isn't listening; it's that the message is communicated inappropriately.

Continuing on this theme, as adults, there's a difference between acting and thinking. For example, if someone tells you, "Don't jump," your reasoning tells you not to jump. But when someone says, "Don't think about... (something)," you inevitably think about it. Remember when I told you, "Don't think about the number two"? I'm sure you'd already thought about it by the time you read or heard that.

Based on this, I pose a question to you: If our prayers are thoughts, how should we pray?

CHAPTER 21

PRAYER AND THE LAW OF ATTRACTION

L et's look at how prayer and the law of attraction work. But first, I want to expand on the elements of prayer. It consists of three elements:

1. **Thought:** involves visualizing the desire of the prayer.

2. **Attention:** refers to the strength and direction of your energy toward your desire, to whom or what you are sending your request and with what intensity.

3. **Intention:** is the type of desire and the result you are looking for, which can be good or bad.

In addition to thought, attention, and intention, another essential element of prayer is the spoken word. Praying out loud has a much deeper spiritual and energetic impact than simply thinking in silence. The words we speak have the power to create or destroy, to bring life or death, as Scripture teaches: "Death and life are in the power of the tongue, and those who love it will eat its fruit" (Proverbs 18:21).

When we pray, we are not just sending thoughts to heaven—we are declaring with spiritual authority. Jesus Himself taught us to speak to the mountain, not merely wish for it to move:

> "Truly I tell you, if anyone says to this mountain, 'Go, throw yourself into the sea,' and does not doubt in their heart but *believes that what they say will happen*, it will be done for them." (Mark 11:23)

The apostle Paul also emphasized that verbal confession is key to salvation:

> "If you declare with your mouth, 'Jesus is Lord,' and believe in your heart that God raised him from the dead, you will be saved. For it is with your heart that you believe and are justified, and it is with your mouth that you profess your faith and are saved." (Romans 10:9–10)

It's not enough to have faith in the heart—we must activate it with our voice. When we declare our prayers out loud, we are using the creative power God has given us as His children. Remember that God created the universe by speaking it into existence (Genesis 1), and we, made in His image, are also called to create with our words.

> "But I tell you that everyone will have to give account on the day of judgment for every empty word they have spoken. For by your words you will be acquitted, and by your words you will be condemned." (Matthew 12:36–37)

Spoken prayer not only expresses faith—it shapes spiritual and material reality. Just as the tongue can set a great forest ablaze (James 3), our words of faith can activate miracles: "Likewise, the tongue is a small part of the body, but it makes great boasts. Consider what a great forest is set on fire by a small spark" (James 3:5).

That's why, when we pray, we must not only focus our thoughts and intentions—but also *speak our faith aloud*, knowing that our words carry power in the spiritual realm.

Now, let me teach you the following teachings.

Mark 11:24 tells us: "Therefore I tell you, whatever you ask for in prayer, *believe that you have received it, and it will be yours.*"

Matthew 21:22 also tells us: "*If you believe, you will receive* whatever you ask for in prayer."

I would emphasize these key words: "believe that you have received it, and it will be yours" and "if you believe, you will receive."

So why do they tell us to ask for what we lack? If we ask for what we lack, we are not believing that we have already received it. This is precisely the opposite of what we read in the gospels of Mark and Matthew, which teach that we must firmly believe that we already have it in order to receive it. In other words, they teach us to have faith and to trust that, if we believe with conviction, the energy of the Holy Spirit will respond to our intention. However, it is important to remember that God's timing is different from ours. He knows when and how to give us things, because we must first live experiences that make us grow spiritually and as people.

Reflecting on this, I have come to the following conclusion: if our thoughts are "energy," if the mind does not distinguish between negative and positive thoughts, and if prayer is, in essence, thought, then by praying focused on our shortcomings, we are not believing that we have already received it.

On the other hand, when we pray out loud as if we already have what we asked for, we are sending a clear signal to God about what we want to attract. As Saint Mark says, "Believe that you have received, and it will be yours," or, as Matthew mentions, "If you believe, you will receive." This relates to the fact that the mind doesn't recognize negative things, as I mentioned in the chapter "The Art of Positive Speaking." Therefore, it's important to pray with faith, visualizing as if we already have it. We must act as if we already possess it to finally obtain it. Changing this mindset can be complicated, but it's crucial. We have to break automatic negative thought patterns that we've developed throughout our lives.

The devil, aware of how our mind works, seeks to focus our attention on our shortcomings and worries. He knows that as long as we remain trapped in this scarcity mentality, it will be much more difficult for us to achieve what we long for. Therefore, it is essential to keep our attention on God's abundance and promises, trusting fully in His power and love to meet our needs. Because without this connection with God, our actions lose meaning.

Imagine this: when you decide to raise your right arm, your brain sends an energetic signal to your arm, and it immediately rises. It's the perfect connection between your brain and your body parts. Now, what happens if that connection is broken or malfunctions? Your arm won't move as it should, no matter how hard you try.

Similarly, our soul, that divine spark within us, has the capacity to be directly connected to the Creator. So why not apply the same logic to prayer? The key is to establish and strengthen that connection with God through the Holy Spirit. It is through this connection that our prayers can be truly effective, believing with faith and certainty that we have already received what we ask for, just as Jesus taught us.

Before praying, let us connect with God by giving thanks, as we are told in Philippians 4:6, "Do not be anxious about anything, but in every situation, by prayer and petition, *with thanksgiving,* present your requests to God."

Then, during your prayer, visualize your request and speak it out loud as if you had already received it, giving thanks to God with faith and conviction. This is like believing it to the fullest. When you receive something, it's natural to give thanks, right? Well, in this case, thank God because you've already received what you're praying for. Visualize yourself receiving what you asked for and perceive the feeling of that request in your body once you've visualized it. This is part of believing with your whole being that it's already yours. For example, if you're facing an illness or discomfort, during prayer, imagine your body healthy and free. Feel the sensation of having a healthy body in your body and thank God that you are free from the illness or discomfort. Then, when you finish the prayer, act as if you already have a healthy body, because you must believe in it. You'll see that, over time, your body will respond and truly heal.

Without a genuine connection to God, our prayers may seem unanswered, not because God doesn't want to answer, but because communication isn't effective. Before praying, it's essential to begin with gratitude, expressing love and compassion, because God is love. This act not only opens our hearts but also establishes a sincere connection with Him.

At the end of the prayer, conclude with the words: "I ask (or thank) you in the name of Jesus." This instruction, which Jesus left us in the Gospel of John (14:12-14), underlines the power of His name:

"Very truly I tell you, whoever believes in me will do the works I have been doing, and they will do even greater

things than these, because I am going to the Father. *And
I will do whatever you ask in my name,* so that the Father
may be glorified in the Son. You may ask me for anything
in my name, and I will do it."

By following this model of prayer, we ensure that our words not
only reach God, but also reflect our faith, love, and trust in His power
to act in our lives and in the lives of others.

Delegating complete control of our lives to God, while being
responsible for our decisions, creates a perfect balance: we act with
faith and trust, allowing His will and purpose to be manifested in us.

Even negative experiences have a purpose: they are lessons designed
to shape us, strengthen us, and draw us closer to God. Instead of
seeing them as insurmountable obstacles, we can recognize them as
divine opportunities to grow, adjust our perspective, and renew our
faith. In this way, our lives flow with greater harmony and purpose,
because we fully trust that everything happens for our good and the
fulfillment of His perfect plan.

When we try to denied our experiences, we are closing the door to
the opportunities God gives us to grow. These lessons, though sometimes difficult, are part of God's plan to refine us and draw us closer to
Him. By ignoring them, we not only delay our spiritual progress, but
we also show God that we don't fully trust His purpose for our lives.

It's essential to remember that God doesn't present us with trials
we can't overcome. Every experience, good or bad, is an opportunity
to strengthen our faith, learn humility, and develop virtues such as
patience, compassion, and perseverance.

By adopting this perspective, our requests are not just personal
desires, but expressions of a life aligned with divine purpose.

Finally, when we face negative thoughts or emotions, we must recognize that they are distractions seeking to distance us from God and our inner peace. By surrendering them to Jesus, as suggested in 2 Corinthians 10:5, we can experience profound liberation.

2 Corinthians 10:5 says, "We demolish arguments and every pretension that sets itself up against the knowledge of God, and *we take captive every thought to make it obedient to Christ.*"

• • •

Some methods to help attract your prayers:

Releasing: Let go of everything you desire in your prayer and allow God to guide you. Consciously focus on what you want and then let it go with thanksgiving. Allow the Holy Spirit to take care of guiding you on the best path you need to live. Release yourself and allow God to guide you day by day, trusting that His divinity will lead you on the best path. When you surrender your being, your body and soul to God and relax, trusting in Him, you will realize that what you once pursued is now following you. The energy of desire, which sometimes causes stress when pursuing what you long for, is what can block things from happening. Once you release it and let go of it with thanksgiving, that's when what you prayed comes to you.

Willpower: Define a goal and move toward it despite any difficulties or obstacles that may arise. This method requires focus, persistence, and seeing problems and difficulties not as obstacles, but as part of the path you need to take to learn. An example here is repetition in learning something, such as exercising to build muscle.

Paired Energy: To attract what you desire in harmony with God's will, you need to align yourself with Him and live according to His principles. If you desire abundance, for example, you must live with generosity and gratitude, knowing that everything you have comes from His grace. Act with humility and love, reflecting the character of Christ in everything you do. If you long for love and compassion, cultivate these virtues in your daily life, following the example of Jesus, who taught us to love one another as He loves us.

If your desire is to find a job or a specific position, act with faith and confidence that God has a plan for you, living with integrity, responsibility, and dedication in everything you undertake. Do so with the certainty that He will guide you toward the right path, according to His will. Visualize and pray as if you have already received what you ask for, firmly believing that He will fulfill His promise, as Jesus says in Saint Mark gospel: "Believe that you have received it, and it will be yours."

Allow Him to transform your thoughts, attitudes, and actions to reflect His love and purpose. As you align yourself with God's will, you will see how what you long for manifests in your life, not by your own strength, but by God's grace at work within you.

CHAPTER 22

ATTENTION: THE POWER OF YOUR PRAYER

Where you put your attention is where your energy is.

In recent years, quantum physics has revealed a reality far more complex and mysterious than traditional science imagined. It has demonstrated that matter and energy are deeply interconnected, and that the simple act of observation can influence the behavior of particles.

One of the best-known studies is the double-slit experiment. In this experiment, a beam of particles—such as electrons or photons—is fired toward a barrier with two slits. If their behavior is observed as they pass through, they act like individual particles. But if they are not observed, they behave like waves, creating an interference pattern. This phenomenon reveals that particles can exist in multiple states until they are observed: this is the so-called observer effect.

This leads us to a surprising premise: observation—or attention—can affect the state of matter. And if we are made of particles, doesn't that mean our attention could also influence our environment, our bodies, and our spiritual reality?

This idea, although viewed skeptically by mainstream scientific circles, has a clear parallel with miracles. When we pray, we do so with thought, attention, and intention. These three elements activate something greater: Divine intervention. The greater the attention and intention, the greater the faith… and the more powerful the prayer.

Christian history is full of examples of transformative collective prayer. Where many people pray fervently, God's presence is powerfully manifested. Places like St. Peter's Basilica in Rome—although Jesus was never physically there—radiate a special energy from centuries of concentrated prayer. It is the accumulated spiritual attention of millions of souls who have surrendered to God in that place.

This helps us better understand the initial statement: where you direct your attention, there your energy flows. Therefore, during the consecration of the host, the priest focuses his mind, intention, and attention on invoking the Holy Spirit. This act transforms the bread into the Body of Christ. It is not just a ritual: it is an explosion of Divine energy when the spiritual and the physical meet in a sacred moment.

ATTENTION, WHEN COMBINED WITH FAITH, CAN MOVE MOUNTAINS.

Another fascinating experiment that reinforces this idea was conducted by Dr. René Peoc'h in 1986. In his doctoral thesis, Peoc'h trained newborn chicks to recognize a robot as their "mother" by means of the phenomenon of imprinting. He then placed the chicks in a cage and allowed the robot—programmed to move randomly—to roam freely. Surprisingly, the robot spent more time near the chicks than would be expected by pure chance, suggesting that the chicks were somehow influencing the robot by attracting it to them.

Dr. Peoc'h concluded that the chickens were able to influence the robot's movement, even when it had no defined pattern.

If chickens can influence a robot through their desire for closeness, how much more can we, as heirs of God, transform our environment through focused intention and prayer?

As Paul reminds us in Romans 8:17:

> "Now if we are children, then we are heirs—heirs of God and co-heirs with Christ, if indeed we share in his sufferings in order that we may also share in his glory" (Romans 8:17).

Among the three elements that constitute prayer, if we lack attention, the intention is weakened. We may have the thought (I want to pray) and the intention (I want to ask for something), but if our attention is scattered, the prayer doesn't reach God with faith. Therefore, attention is the backbone of powerful prayer. And this only has a real effect if we are connected to the Holy Spirit. Otherwise, it's like a signal without a receiver.

My purpose in this chapter is to emphasize that attention is energy. If we direct our energy toward God, with intention and faith, we not only change our lives… we can open the door to miracles.

In the modern world, especially in competitive environments, attention is synonymous with perseverance: focusing without distraction, acting with presence and determination. This principle, when applied to the spiritual realm, becomes even more powerful: focusing on God, persevering in prayer, remaining attentive to the present, the "here and now," and allowing His will to act.

Your attention is not just mental focus; it's a stream of spiritual energy that, when combined with faith and the power of the Holy Spirit, can move heaven in your favor. Wherever you place your attention with intention, there God can work. Just as Jesus healed with a word or a look, you too, as a child of God, can direct your energy toward love, healing, and divine will.

Focused attention is the channel through which the power of prayer flows.

> *"And these signs will accompany those who believe: In my name they will drive out demons; they will speak in new tongues; they will pick up snakes with their hands; and when they drink deadly poison, it will not hurt them at all; they will place their hands on sick people, and they will get well."* (Mark 16:17-18)

CHAPTER 23

THE TRUE BATTLE

Psychologists teach that we shouldn't label people, especially children. If a child behaves inappropriately, instead of saying "You're unbearable," the correct thing to do is point out the behavior: "Your attitude is unbearable." This distinction is key. When someone is judged by what they do and not by who they are, their identity is protected and the door is opened to change.

Words have power. If a child is constantly told they're "clumsy" or "bad," they'll grow to believe it. On the other hand, if you simply point out their behavior, they'll understand that their actions can be improved, without it defining who they are.

This principle doesn't just apply to parenting. It's also a spiritual key, because behind every person is an identity in the making. When we harshly label someone, we not only hurt them, but we also help reinforce a lie: the one that says that person *is* what they did wrong.

So what does this have to do with God?

The answer lies in what Jesus revealed: our true struggle is not against people, but against the evil powers that influence them. In Ephesians 6:12 we read:

"For our struggle is not against flesh and blood, but against the rulers, against the authorities, against the powers of this dark world and against the spiritual forces of evil in the heavenly realms."

Jesus knew this. That's why, when he saw someone possessed or enslaved by evil, he didn't condemn them but rather expelled the demon. He knew that behind sin there was a wound, and behind that wound a lie sown by the enemy.

In some cases, Jesus even addressed the spirit by the name of its manifestation. For example, when he encountered a boy possessed and unable to speak or hear, he rebuked the spirit saying, "You deaf and mute spirit," he said, "I command you, come out of him and never enter him again" (Mark 9:25). This shows that demons often operate through specific patterns of oppression—some cause sickness, others emotional bondage, confusion, hatred, or division. Jesus discerned the spiritual root behind the behavior and dealt directly with that spirit, not the person. He came to set the captives free, not to accuse them.

Satan works like this: first, he hurts a person and drives them to act badly. Then, he incites the person who is hurt to reject, judge, and label them. In this way, he sows division, resentment, and rift among brothers and sisters. He makes us fight, when the real battle is spiritual.

That's why Jesus asks us to put on the armor of God: to resist temptations and maintain peace, even when others offend us. It's not about allowing evil, but about knowing how to confront it from the Spirit. When Jesus was arrested, one of his disciples drew his sword. But he stopped him. Jesus's fight was not against men, but against the sin and lies that ruled them.

If we attack those who hurt us with insults, we only strengthen the enemy's chains. By telling someone they're "weak," "ridiculous," or "unintelligible," we are collaborating with the lie the devil wants to implant in their identity.

Jesus came to restore that identity. His mission was to remind us that we are children of God, called to live in love and truth. And if we want to be His disciples, we must learn to separate the sin from the sinner, the act from the person, the error from the essence.

What many psychologists and experts teach today, Jesus already said it. His word is full of wisdom about human nature, inner healing, and the power of nonjudgment. We just need to learn to read it with the eyes of the soul.

> *"Be merciful, just as your Father is merciful. Do not judge, and you will not be judged. Do not condemn, and you will not be condemned. Forgive, and you will be forgiven. Give, and it will be given to you. A good measure, pressed down, shaken together and running over, will be poured into your lap. For with the measure you use, it will be measured to you."* (Luke 6:36-38)

CHAPTER 24

THE POWER
OF BLESSING

"When he was at the table with them, he took bread,
gave thanks, broke it and began to give it to them."

LUKE 24:30

As a child, I grew up in a family where blessing food before eating was a daily custom. Back then, I did it out of routine. I didn't understand its true meaning, nor the spiritual power behind the gesture. Over time, the practice faded away. I no longer saw it as necessary and simply forgot about it.

Everything changed when I began to understand the nature of the power of our words. I learned that everything in the universe—people, animals, plants, food, objects—is made of energy. I also discovered that gratitude and positive words are not just kind expressions, but vibrations that directly affect matter and spirit.

One of the studies that impacted me the most was that of Dr. Masaru Emoto, author of *The Message of Water*. In his studies, Emoto shows that water responds to our words and intentions. When phrases like "Thank you" or "I love you" were uttered over containers of water, the crystals that formed were harmonious and beautiful when viewed under a microscope. By contrast, when words like "I hate you" or "war" were used, the crystals were chaotic and misshapen.

This phenomenon has also been replicated in plants: when they receive kind words, they grow stronger; but if they are exposed to insults or contempt, their development is affected. The reason? Our words are not just sounds, but carriers of energy. And since everything in the universe is energy, what we say has a real impact.

This led me to a powerful conclusion: if our words can affect water, and if our bodies are mostly made up of water—up to 70% in children—then our words also profoundly affect our physical, emotional, and spiritual health.

Even more surprising was the discovery that water blessed in places of prayer—temples, sacred rivers, pilgrimages—presents harmonious crystals similar to those generated by positive words. It's as if the prayers have imbued the water with divine energy, transforming it into something healing.

Then I understood why Jesus blessed food, why priests bless our homes, and why our words have so much power. This isn't a simple symbolic act: we are transferring energy, invoking protection, and transforming the ordinary into something spiritual.

"In the beginning was the Word, and the Word was with God, and the Word was God. He was with God in the beginning. Through him all things were made; without him nothing was made that has been made... The Word became flesh and made his dwelling among us." (John 1:1-3,14)

Jesus is the Word made flesh. His energy is the purest and most powerful. Therefore, when we bless in his name, we are invoking that

Divine energy that transforms and purifies. If something has been touched by negative or demonic energy, only the presence of Christ can completely cleanse it.

This led me not only to bless food again, but also to do so with intention, awareness, and faith. This is because by giving thanks, we also protect. And by invoking the name of Jesus, we transform the ordinary into something sacred.

Furthermore, I understood that blessing shouldn't be limited to food alone. We can bless our home, our children, our car, our body, our words—anything that's part of our lives.

Every positive word is a seed of light; every negative word, a shadow that clouds the soul. As a father, I am aware that my words to my children build their internal energy. Their bodies, so full of water, react to what they hear, feel, and believe. That's why blessing them with love, even in difficult times, is one of the greatest responsibilities I have.

This is how I understood that blessing isn't a religious obligation. It's a spiritual tool. A way to protect, give thanks, transform, and uplift.

May our words, thoughts, and prayers always be filled with light. When we bless food, may we do so not out of routine, but with awareness. For when we invoke the name of Jesus, we don't just give thanks: we bring His presence into the moment, and with it, His peace, His protection, and His love.

PRAYER TO BLESS FOOD

Lord Jesus, I thank you for this food, for your provision, for your love, and for your faithfulness. In your name I bless them, and I declare that they are full of life, health, and strength. Purify everything that does not come from you and make this food a means of healing for my body and soul. I invite you to this table and I give you the glory. Amen.

CHAPTER 25

THE ENEMY'S SILENT TRAP

✝

You may believe you are free, that your decisions are yours, and that you choose your path. But what if I told you that, without realizing it, you are walking along paths carved out by forces that seek to disconnect you from God? Not with visible chains, but with routines, distractions, and subtle lies. This is the enemy's silent trap. This is his Matrix.

WHAT IS THE MATRIX?

Beyond the popular idea of a simulation, the Matrix represents a system of automatic behaviors, unconscious habits, and mechanical reactions that govern our lives. It's like living on autopilot, without stopping to reflect, without making conscious decisions. The more trapped we are in this system, the further we drift away from the purpose for which we were created.

THE GIFT OF FREE WILL

God gave us a sacred gift: the ability to choose freely. But when we live under unconscious habits—guided by our environment, unhealed traumas, or empty routines—that gift is diluted. We stop acting with intention and become reactive. We lose true freedom: the freedom to choose what is good, what is just, what is divine.

WE LIVE ON AUTOMATIC

Most people act like this every day. From the moment they wake up until they go to sleep, they repeat routines without question:

- They unlock the cell phone without thinking.

- They get upset when criticized without thinking.

- They react as they learned, without deciding how they want to respond.

Does this sound familiar?

As children, we learned to behave by imitating our parents or caregivers. This repetition created internal programming that we continue to reproduce generation after generation.

But living on autopilot isn't living. It's still asleep inside the Matrix.

DO YOU HAVE FREE WILL?

To regain control, you have to *raise your awareness.* Here are some practical ways to get started:

- Change your daily routes to break the routine.

- Set alarms that remind you to take conscious breaks.

- Reduce your use of social media: it's a tool of the modern Matrix to steal your attention.

- Make conscious choices even in small actions, like opening a door.

- Practice Christian prayer and meditation, which train the mind to discern and connect with God.

For example, I had the habit of grabbing my phone every time I went to the bathroom. One day, I deleted a social media app. The next time I went, my hand went straight to my phone, but I remembered I no longer had the app. I smiled. That small moment was an act of consciousness. I stepped out of the Matrix, even if it was just for a moment.

KEEP YOUR EYES ON JESUS

The Matrix wants to distract you from Jesus. It succeeded with Peter at sea:

In Matthew 14:28-31, Peter walks on the water when his eyes are fixed on Jesus. But when he focuses on the waves and the wind, he becomes afraid... and begins to sink.

Likewise, when we take our eyes off Jesus and focus on distraction, fear, or worry, we begin to sink into chaos. But Jesus always reaches out to lift us up. We just have to look at him again.

THE SPIRITUAL ORIGIN OF THE MATRIX

This system isn't just psychological. It has a spiritual origin. The devil seeks to keep us trapped in automatisms, distractions, and negative emotions: anxiety, stress, envy, superficiality. He even uses tools like social media to steal our attention and distance us from our soul.

The first step to breaking this trap is to live mindfully. Ask yourself:

Does what I consume bring me closer to peace… or chaos?

Does this habit bring me closer to Jesus… or push me away?

INHERITED LOADS

Since Adam and Eve, humanity has been attacked by the enemy's deception. The consequences of original sin, although forgiven by Christ, continue to manifest themselves in the form of destructive family patterns, emotional wounds, or repetitive behaviors. We do not inherit sin, but we do inherit the *wounds of the soul* that must be healed and rejected in the name of Jesus.

BREAK THE CHAINS OF THE MATRIX

The Matrix is the devil's constant attempt to keep us trapped in unconsciousness. But you can escape. By awakening your consciousness and keeping your gaze on God, you regain your *spiritual freedom* and your true identity as a child of God.

The devil only has power if you give him permission to enter your mind.

The devil doesn't need to scream to dominate you; he just needs to keep you from waking up. But when you fix your eyes on Jesus, the veil falls away, the truth is revealed, and freedom begins.

CHAPTER 26

THE COSMIC DISGUISE OF THE ENEMY

Astrology maintains that the positions of the stars influence our personality and destiny. Many people, searching for answers, turn to it as a guide. But as Christians, we must remember that only God has a perfect plan for our lives. "For I know the plans I have for you," declares the Lord, "*plans to prosper you and not to harm you, plans to give you hope and a future*" (Jeremiah 29:11).

LOOKING FOR ANSWERS IN THE WRONG PLACE

For a time in my life, I was also drawn to astrology. Some things about it seemed to make sense. But I soon realized that these outside influences were not only limiting, but were distancing me from God. Our soul doesn't belong to the universe, the stars, or a birth chart. Our soul belongs to the Creator.

And how does this distance us from God? It's simple: when you turn to horoscopes or seek guidance from the planets, you divert your gaze from the One who can truly guide you. You are placing your trust in creation, not in the Creator.

CREATION IS NOT CONSULTED, THE CREATOR IS CONSULTED.

The enemy knows this. That's why his strategy is subtle: to distract you. To make you believe that God is distant or unresponsive, so that you seek answers in the immediate, the visible, the popular. Horoscopes, numerology, and card readings are spiritual lures. But God is always willing to guide you, if you choose to listen.

The stars, though beautiful, only reflect God's greatness. They don't govern your life. They don't decide your future. They didn't write your story. God did.

> "Come to me, all you who are weary and burdened, and
> I will give you rest." (Matthew 11:28)

Instead of turning to impersonal forces, turn to the one who created you out of love, who knows you by name, and who does have an eternal purpose for you.

> *"No wise man, enchanter, magician or diviner can explain to*
> *the king the mystery he has asked about, but there is a God*
> *in heaven who reveals mysteries."* (Daniel 2:27-28)

DON'T GET CARRIED AWAY BY THE CURRENT

Imagine you're floating on a board in the middle of the sea, without paddling. Where does the current take you? Exactly: somewhere you didn't decide.

This is what happens when you live without intention, without conscience, without God. You're swept away by the rhythm of the world, trends, social media, opinions. Before you know it, you're far from your purpose.

That state of apathy and spiritual disconnection is part of the Matrix. The enemy doesn't need to chain you physically; he just needs you to live without direction.

But God did not create us for passivity, but to walk in His light and make decisions guided by His Spirit. "Even though I walk through the darkest valley, I will fear no evil, for you are with me." (Psalm 23)

Jesus doesn't just calm physical storms; He also calms the noise of your thoughts, the uncertainty of tomorrow, and the lies the world tries to spread.

When you give Him the helm of your life, you no longer drift. Jesus becomes the captain of your boat, always guiding you toward a safe harbor: His will and His eternal love.

TIME: THE INVISIBLE TYRANT

We live under the invisible yoke of a master who never rests: time. Not time as a gift from God, but as a system imposed by man, quantified in seconds, minutes, and hours, and governed by the clock.

The clock—a human invention—was born to organize our lives, but ended up enslaving us. Ever since humans decided to measure time, they turned it into a ruthless dictator: it controls our decisions, defines our limits, and conditions our emotions. But what exactly are we measuring?

Time is "the duration of things subject to change." But if the soul is eternal, and change and death do not exist in it, why do we live as if every second defines our worth?

From the beginning, human beings observed the cycles of the sun and moon to guide their activities. The Babylonians, Egyptians, and Greeks divided the day, first into mornings and evenings, then into hours and minutes. This is how instruments like the clepsydra and the hourglass emerged, leading to the modern clock. And with each advance, we lost freedom.

To understand how we have changed, I want to share two scenes with you:

LIFE UNDER THE SUNLIGHT

A merchant wakes up with the first rays of the sun. There's no alarm, just the birdsong. He has breakfast with his family, greets his neighbors, and walks to the market when the sun is high. He buys, sells, talks, and shares. He returns home at dusk and goes to bed when the sun sets. His clock is the sky. His guide, the light.

LIFE UNDER THE DICTATORSHIP OF TIME

Another businessman wakes up when his alarm goes off. He looks at his clock: 6:30. He runs. The kids run. The wife leaves without breakfast. He arrives at work. Meetings, schedules, pressures. Calls, tasks, traffic. He returns at night, have dinner, set the alarm…and repeat. His guide is the clock; his pressure, time.

The difference is clear: one lives; the other survives.

I experienced this myself. I once went camping with my son in a forest without a clock, without electricity, without a cell phone. We woke up with the light, ate when we were hungry, talked without looking at the time. There I discovered the peace of the present. Without haste, without stress. My soul breathed.

That trip made me understand that true freedom isn't in doing more things…but in stopping running.

God doesn't measure your worth in minutes. He didn't create you to run after the clock, but to walk with Him, in the here and now. That's why Jesus prayed at dawn and dusk. He lived in connection with the Father's rhythm, not with the human ticking.

It's not about eliminating clocks, but about not letting them define your existence. Make space for silence, contemplation, the joy of being. Stop measuring your life by what you do and start valuing it for who you are: a child of God, eternal like your soul.

Pause. Look at the sky. Listen to your soul.

Will you continue to live under the dictatorship of time... or under the light of the Spirit?

CHAPTER 28

THE NOW WHERE FAITH DWELLS

Yesterday is history, the future is a mystery, and today is a gift, that's why it's called the present." This powerful phrase reflects a profound truth that aligns perfectly with Jesus's words in Matthew 6:34: *"Therefore do not worry about tomorrow, for tomorrow will worry about itself. Each day has enough trouble of its own."*

The now is the greatest gift God has given us. It is the only moment in which we can act, decide, pray, forgive, and love. And yet, how often do we get lost in the "what ifs" of the past or the "what will happens" of the future? The mind, when not centered on God, becomes a factory of worries. The fear of tomorrow and the burden of yesterday rob us of the peace that only exists in the present.

God dwells in the now. He is not a God of "yesterday" or a God of "perhaps tomorrow." His Spirit acts in the present moment, waiting for us to seek Him here, where we are truly alive.

But society has distracted us. We live with our phones in hand, rushing from one commitment to the next, planning, remembering, comparing. Even in intimate moments—like sharing a meal or playing with our children—we are absent. Our attention is elsewhere.

Living in a hurry is a modern form of slavery. It's true that we must plan, but not at the cost of missing out on the present. As Isaiah 43:18-19 says: "Don't remember yesterday, don't think about the past. I am going to do something new, and you will see that it will appear right now. I will open a path in the desert and rivers in the barren land."

God is always doing something new. But only if we are present can we notice it.

Jesus made it clear: "*Come to me, all you who are weary and burdened, and I will give you rest*" (Matthew 11:28).

That rest is now. Not when you've got everything figured out. Not when the weekend arrives. It's today, if you choose to trust.

Every morning is a new opportunity. God extends His hand to walk with you. But if your mind is caught in the pain of the past or the anxiety of the future, you won't be able to grasp it.

Living in the present doesn't mean ignoring responsibilities, but rather surrendering them. It means recognizing that God is in control and that every second can be sacred if we live it with Him.

Even in the midst of challenges, He is at work. As we let go of control, trust, and act from faith, our lives begin to align with His eternal purpose.

Reliving the past prevents us from changing, growing, and evolving because our thoughts and emotions remain trapped in experiences that no longer exist.

Freedom is in the now. Where God awaits you.

> "*The Lord has done it this very day; let us rejoice today and be glad.*" (Psalm 118:24)

CHAPTER 29

WHISPERS FOR THE SOUL

A truly free human being is one who becomes aware of his soul and recognizes his original identity as a child of God, with all the benefits that this entails.

Why should God give you more if you are not grateful for what you already have?

Finding the reason you came to this world should be your first goal in life. The second is fulfilling that purpose.

One of the greatest blessings bestowed upon humankind is the ability to be free. However, even freedom requires limits that respect nature, our neighbors, and our own well-being. Living without limits reflects a neglect of the soul, and a neglected soul cannot reach its full potential.

God's commandments are like a mirror that reveals our spiritual stains. They are not meant to condemn us, but to guide us toward inner cleansing. That "bath" that purifies the soul is Jesus's forgiveness, which we find in confession. Take care of your soul, live with purpose, and open your heart to God's love and forgiveness. Only then can you become the best version of yourself, aligned with His will.

Having no limits is like owning a Lamborghini, driving at 200 km/h, and having no brakes. Soon, we crash.

Many say that a child doesn't choose their parents, but if we believe that the soul is eternal, conscious, and free, couldn't we think that it does choose them? This idea motivates me to be a better parent, because I believe my children chose me for a reason. And that reason commits me to not letting them down.

A materialist isn't someone who desires things, but rather someone who needs them to fill an inner void. They're someone who has strayed from their essence and isn't living their purpose. Therefore, they seek external satisfaction that only comes from doing what they love.

Tell me how much you criticize, and I'll tell you how much you love yourself. Destructive criticism stems from a lack of self-love. Those who value themselves have no need to speak ill of others. Criticism darkens the soul and fuels envy, which ultimately destroys us from within.

Less criticism, more peace. Take care of your soul, and the negative words will fade away on their own.

A NEW BEGINNING

We have reached the end of this Maze.

Thank you for walking through it with me.

Now that you know these truths, walk with faith, with awareness, and with a heart aligned to God's purpose.

May this ending be, in truth, a new beginning: the awakening to your real and divine essence.

And if this book has touched your life, I invite you to leave a review. Your testimony can become the seed that inspires others, so that in their own journey through the maze of beliefs they too may find the Divine Truth.

ABOUT THE AUTHOR

Hector Cantu Kalifa, a child of God, like any other baptized person, has written this book with a single purpose: to bring more people closer to Jesus so they may know His love, His forgiveness, and His Divine energy. All glory belongs to Him; Hector is merely an instrument, a means to explain who we are and who Jesus is.

Hector lives in Monterrey, Mexico, with his wife Paulina, with whom he shares the joy of raising their four children.

If you'd like to contact him, you can email him at hector@hectorcantuk.com or follow him on social media at:

WWW.X.COM/HECTORCANTUK

WWW.INSTAGRAM.COM/HECTORCKALIFA

www.ingramcontent.com/pod-product-compliance
Lightning Source LLC
Chambersburg PA
CBHW071304130626
46556CB00003B/1465